# PAULA ENGBORG

# A WAY UP

## 1 WOMAN ACROSS THE PACIFIC NW

Oil On Water Press

**OIL ON WATER PRESS**
Oxford, UK
First published in 2023
office@oilonwaterpress.com

**A WAY UP**
**1 Woman Across the Pacific NW**

A CIP catalogue record for this book is available from the British Library

ISBN PAPERBACK       978-1-909394-89-6
ISBN E-BOOK          978-1-909394-90-2

ORIGINAL TRUE-LIFE STORIES & MEMOIR

Exclusive content at **OILONWATERPRESS.COM**

"The principal business of life is to enjoy It."
Samuel Butler (1612–1680)

# Contents

I dedicate this book to my sons
Matt, Willy and Max.

# PROLOGUE

||||||||||||||||||||||||||||||||||||||||||||||||||

ALONE ON A rock ledge in the dead of winter, I was stuck. My partner, Chad, had edged out of sight looking for a way down. I glanced back at the icy rocks fifty-feet below and knew we were screwed. My fingertips were getting numb, and I had to find a way up and soon, because my hands wouldn't be useful much longer.

We were members of mountain rescue, and no one would come looking for us for a long, long time. Our two-way radio was lying in the snow at the base of the route, and I was angry and had some thoughts. "Damn, no radio and no rope. Yeah, thanks a lot Chad! If things get worse..." I laughed and said, *"It can't get much worse, dummy! What the hell you gunna do?"*

That day was over twenty years ago. Boy, have things changed! I haven't climbed for years, but I've found new ways to get my kicks. My grandsons probably think baking and gardening are all I've ever done, but I'll rock their little worlds at our next cookout. The boys just might drop their s'mores when I tell them how the grim reaper invited me to come on down.

I smelled snow in the air on my morning walk, and decided to get a hold of Carol. Once back in my warm kitchen, I called her and invited her to go snowshoeing with me. When I hung up the phone, I spooned black tea leaves in a china pot, and put the kettle on, because she lived on the next block. A few minutes later, she rapped on the door, let herself in, and I gave her a big squeeze. She slouched in the kitchen chair, sprawled her legs out, and her pooch Mochi ran down the hall to hang out with my husband, Matt.

Blowing on a steaming cup of tea, Carol asked when and where we'd go. I set a plate of cookies on the table and suggested Hurricane Hill or the Klahhane Ridge sometime in the next few days.

"I'll keep track of the weather and snow conditions, and you'll be safe with me, because I can do an avalanche assessment." Her beautiful almond-shaped eyes widened.

"Wow! You're an avalanche expert?"

"No, not at all, but I can assess the snow for safety."

"So, you must be a mountain climber."

"I was, a long time ago. I have a climbing journal — wanna see some pictures?"

"Yeah, go get it."

I ran upstairs and blew the dust off the journal. Then I headed back down and handed it to Carol. She flipped through the pages and looked at it with her fresh-from-the-East Coast perspective, and snapped bolt upright in her chair. She blurted out "You're a wild ass!"

We talked about some of the things I did when I was a climber, and she said I should write a book about it. I told her, "That was a long time ago, and I'm not a writer." After she'd gone I wondered if I should give that a try, but I had doubts. I sat down at my desk with the journal on my lap and gazed across the water at Mt. Rainier. I felt a tug, was pulled into the past, and began to type this story.

# THE MOUNTAIN

IIIIIIIIIIIIIIIIIIIIIIIIIIIIIIIIIIIIIIIIIIIIIIIIIIIIIIIIIIIIIIIIIIIII

IN THE SPRING of 1999, I was on my way out of the gym on Bainbridge Island and almost collided with my buddy Clay. A few years before Clay had taught me how to swim laps. He told me his friend, Cebe, wanted to meet me, and gave me an unusual description of him. "Cebe is a top-notch climber, an instructor for the Seattle Mountaineers, and one of the authors in the climber's bible *Freedom of the Hills*." Cebe was also a member of the health club who had apparently noticed me, even though I hadn't noticed him. At that time, even though I stood just 5'4" tall, I was in tip-top shape, with a muscular build, and had established a reputation in the community as a top-notch fitness trainer.

"That's great! Please tell him I'll meet him here tomorrow at noon. I've gotta go. I'm running late."

I jogged to the Streamliner Diner to have lunch with my friend Tom, and thought, "Huh, that was weird. All that mountain stuff makes no sense. Why should I care about that guy's hobbies? Clay said it's a big deal or something. I don't get it." I spotted Tom having a smoke, and poof! all those thoughts just vanished.

The next day when I met Cebe, he asked me if I'd like to join his climb on Mount Rainier. Initially I was surprised by that invitation, and then a brilliant idea popped into my head. I told him I'd like to go, and asked if I could bring my friend Jenny. Cebe said she could go if I thought she was strong enough. We talked about the trip for a while, and I sussed out that fitness was the deciding factor and having no experience wasn't a deal breaker.

Cebe needed one more person on the climb, and asked if I could find a strong candidate. As a personal trainer, I was acquainted with a lot of fit people in the community, and he didn't have to ask me twice. It wasn't hard for me to think of men who were strong enough to climb a mountain, because even though I had no interest in climbing, I had plenty of interest in the opposite sex. I was a divorced woman hoping to remarry some day, and there were some guys in the gym I wouldn't mind sharing a tent with!

Naturally the first man I approached was Troy. He had a body to die for. The last time I talked to him, I'd hired him to teach strength training to my son Max. I invited him to go, and was disappointed when he said he didn't think he could do it. I was surprised too because he was built like a brick house. He explained that his cardiovascular fitness wasn't the best because he was training for a bodybuilding contest. That didn't daunt me, and I said that he had two months to work on cardio. He had no interest at all in climbing. Well, I could understand that, because I didn't really have much interest in it either, but thought I had a good spiel.

A couple minutes later, I saw Gary doing lunges with dumbbells. He was married and younger than me, but he had a nice body and trained hard. I had my fingers crossed when I asked him to climb Mt. Rainier, and he said yes right on the spot. That was good news, and it only took me ten minutes to complete my task.

The next day, I could hardly wait to see Jenny, and paced nervously all over the gym. I'd never had any interest in climbing, but Mt. Rainier was on her bucket list. I couldn't wait to see her reaction. I wondered if she'd scream or pee her pants.

I tried to hold back a little longer and started her on a leg workout, but after she finished I couldn't hold out anymore.

"Jenny, I've been invited to climb Mt. Rainier and you're invited too!" Oddly, her expression didn't change at all, and my bubble of joy was punctured and rapidly deflating.

"Who Invited you?"

"A mountaineer named Cebe."

"I'd like to meet him and find out about his qualifications and experience."

"Okay, I'll give you his phone number when we're done."

That was the end of that conversation. Her reaction, or better yet, the lack of one was a real letdown, and she was so leery. At her next workout, she'd done a 180 and was excited about climbing Mt. Rainier.

Jenny was planning on going, and I was thinking about leaving. Since she was a confirmed member of the climbing party, I'd accomplished my mission. I thought climbing looked boring and tedious, but I was curious about it too, and decided to tag along on the training climb. If I didn't like it, as I suspected, I'd find someone to take my place.

When I was 13, I climbed up in the hayloft to take a look around. What I saw up there didn't amount to much, just bales of hay. I heard my horse Zack whinny in his stall below. After I checked it out up there, it turned into my favorite hideout. It was a great place to read, and sometimes the best place to escape from Mom and Dad when they were fighting. Mom had a wicked arm and tended to throw things at Dad, so the hayloft kept me out of her line of fire. The training climb on Mt. Washington would be more difficult than climbing into a hayloft, but I thought I'd give it a try.

The weather was so crappy at Mt. Washington that I wouldn't even bother going for a hike on a day like that now. It was miserably cold and foggy, and I couldn't wait to get moving and warm up. All we saw from the logging road was a thick pine forest obscured by low clouds and heavy fog drifting through the woods. Most of the people in our group didn't know each other, but a steady chatter filled the air. The landmarks were covered with deep snow, so Cebe picked an opening in the trees, and we plunged in. It was hard to see anything at all in that damn fog, so we just flailed on up through the forest.

After we cleared the woods, we came to the base of an avalanche chute that shot nearly straight up the side of that mountain. Cebe said it was stable, but I had an unsettling view of avalanche debris. The snow was roughed up and looked like it had just been poured out of a dump truck, with big branches and tree bits sticking out of it. Everyone blithely marched up that slope, so I followed.

About midway up the chute was a really deep moat. I heard water running way down at the bottom of it. That got me worried and Cebe's comments on the way up there hadn't helped one bit. He'd said when people fall into a crevasse on a glacier and disappear sometimes they turn up in a river years later. That was not heartwarming information, and my general concern became active from then on. I had the image of my desiccated, ice-encrusted body in mind. Cebe anchored a rope so we could prusik up a nearly vertical wall of snow above the moat. A prusik knot can be used to ascend a rope. It's easy to loosen and slide up the rope, then tighten again. I was thinking that we weren't on a glacier, but if I fell into that moat I might disappear.

I watched people rely on something that looked like a piece of shoelace to hold their body weight. That looked scary, but I learned how to use the prusik knot and worked my way up that rope as fast as I could. I'd had a bad attitude all day and was pretty sure I wasn't cut out for this crap, until I stood at the top of the chute. Initially when I looked into the moat I was afraid and wanted to go home, but standing above it, I felt like I'd really accomplished something big and was on cloud nine.

There was no visibility, because we were socked in by clouds at the top of Washington, and everyone crammed into the small crater on the summit; everyone but me. I thought it looked too crowded in there, but the others urged me to join them, so I reluctantly stepped in. Some photos were snapped as we proudly stood at over 6,000 feet above sea level, and I had a new appreciation for climbing. I reached into my parka, and pulled out a Cadbury Dairy Milk Fruit and Nut chocolate bar and took a big bite. It tasted better than ever and the switch was flipped. I decided then and there that I was all in and couldn't wait to climb Mt. Rainier.

We stopped on the way down, and I turned to watch Cebe bringing up the rear. He took huge plunging steps that made each boot print about a yard apart. He moved swiftly down that steep snowy mountainside and reminded me of a superhero in action.

My dad had been a super athlete when he was a member of the Brooklyn Dodgers baseball team. I thought about calling to tell him about Mt. Rainier. We spent an awful lot of time discussing my West Coast versus his East Coast weather and the news of my upcoming climb would certainly enliven our conversation.

By law he was my step-dad, but he'd been the only dad I'd known. He was a very conventional man who'd tried to teach my musically gifted brother to play ball, but Billy dodged the ball instead of catching it. I'd told my dad I wanted to play and he said no, because I could get hurt. I pouted, but he gave me the look and nodded toward the bleachers. All I wanted was to hit the ball and run around the bases so badly that I would've gotten banged up with pleasure. Based on our history I decided not to make that call. Instead I called my hairdresser. I had things to do and people to see, starting with my haircut.

Richard dropped his jaw when I told him to give me a buzz cut and shave the Nike swoosh in the back of my head. He asked why I wanted that hair style. I told him why, and he smiled. "I want a copy of that picture Paula."

"I'll be sure to give you one."

The buzz of the hair clippers filled my ears, and I watched in the mirror as I was transformed from a woman with a golden mane into a tomboy. When it was done, I ran my hand across the top of my head and it felt like silk velvet. Richard handed me a mirror and spun me. "Thanks Richard. Great job." As I hopped out of the chair, he told me not to forget that he wanted a copy of my summit picture.

Hair was the least of my worries and cardiovascular fitness trumped all. On Mt. Rainier, the air gets thinner as you climb higher, and something as simple as walking can be difficult. Only about 50 percent of the people who attempt Rainier make it to the top. Jenny and I needed to be in the half that made it, so I amped up our cardio workouts.

To prepare for the climb, I loaded my backpack, weighed myself and then weighed myself with the pack on to see how much the difference was. It was forty-eight pounds, so I unpacked it and tried to figure out what I could take out. I like to keep things simple, so there wasn't much I could weed out. A picture of my brother Billy encased in plastic from our grandfather's key chain might've weighed an ounce, but I'd vowed to make him a part of that climb.

One of the biggest shocks of my life happened when I was in my twenties. My dad called at four in the morning, so I knew something was wrong, and the thought flashed through my mind that it must be about my mother. When he told me my brother Bill was killed in a car accident that night, I fell apart and had difficulty doing daily tasks for the next week. He was only two years older than me and we were close. I couldn't picture life without him, because whenever I had problems, Billy was on the spot with a solution. Mom died a couple years later, but she'd been a heavy drinker and though I was sad, her death didn't have the same powerful effect on me that my brother's did.

After surveying everything that would go into my pack, including the picture of my brother, I began to reload it, and the phone rang. My dad was on the line calling from Virginia for our weekly chat. I was still afraid to tell him about Rainier, so I didn't mention it. When I returned to repacking my backpack, I made up my mind that it would be best to tell him about the climb after it was over, and worked on the task at hand.

I rolled up my extra pair of long johns army style, stuffed them in the pack, and began to think about when I'd moved here from the East Coast seven years before. I'd injured my knee in a skiing accident and lost my sales job to boot. The recovery from surgery was a long one, and my boss had to fill my position and fired me. I was devastated, because I'd been the top sales rep in that company, and getting fired due to surgery felt like someone had kicked me in the gut.

I was divorced and my son Matt, lived with me in Virginia. I sent him to his dad's in Washington for summer vacation, and toward the end of that summer my ex called and told me Matt wouldn't be returning. He'd missed his brothers and hated living in Virginia. I missed his brothers too, but at the time I had a good job and was in no position to leave. So when I lost that job I had no choice, and I headed west. Reliving this I stuffed all my angst and the sleeping bag into the compression sack and was ready to go.

After I lost my job in Virginia, instead of accepting the new job offer I'd gotten from a local vineyard, I threw my stuff in the car and drove west. That journey was difficult to make, because I had limited resources and had never driven across the country before. My eyes flashed from the road map to the highway so many times I'd wished I could superimpose it on the windshield. I drove 16-18 hours a day in a mad dash to Washington, because I couldn't wait to see my kids.

Dithering over a few small items made me feel pretty stupid. All I was trying to do was pack light and take the bare minimum on this trip. There I was packing for a climb on the tallest mountain in the state of Washington, but couldn't decide if I wanted to take a washcloth or my Altoids. I got tired of wasting time and getting nowhere. I reasoned that the washcloth was light as a feather, and since minty breath was a must for me, I shoved them both in my pack and was done.

# MAKING IT TO THE TOP

||||||||||||||||||||||||||||||||||||||||||||||||||||||||||||||||||||||||||||||||||||||||||

THE TWO MONTHS we had to wait before the big climb whizzed by, and on July 23rd Jenny and I had the jitters as she drove us to Longmire in Mt. Rainier National Park. We spent the night in a lodge there. The next day we got up early and got in the line to pick up the reservations for our climbing party. After that we met with the rest of our group at Paradise, and started up Mt. Rainier around 9:30 in the morning on July 24th, 1999. It was a cloudy, cheerless morning and the sky was a dull gray, but our spirits were high.

The snow on the trail up was compacted because lots of people had gone up before us. I was cold for about the first ten minutes, but hiking uphill with a heavy backpack warmed me up fast. Frank was right in front of me. I'd been introduced to him and his climbing partner right before we began the ascent. He was Cebe's friend from the Mountaineers Club, and was an experienced climb leader who would manage one of the rope teams on the way to the summit. He'd climbed here before, so I asked him, "Why are we all going up on this same path?"

"Sticking to this trail is the safest way to go."

"It doesn't look dangerous to me."

"Some hikers and skiers stray too far from this trail and find themselves tumbling down off the edge of the snowfield."

I'd interrupted him in a conversation with his partner and he seemed a little cranky. There wasn't a lot to see on the Muir Snowfield, but I saw a couple of skiers coming down. Apparently some had skied right off the sides of the snow field! That must have been a big shock when they went from a long, pleasant run into midair.

On one of our many rest stops I began to think about solo climbing, because we were going so slow that we were being passed by other climbing parties. I had no patience and the slow pace aggravated me. At the time I had no idea what a monster my lack of patience would become.

Jenny was the slowest member in our climbing party and that puzzled me. Hiking up the snow field must have been difficult for her, but I couldn't imagine why. As her personal trainer, I knew she had the strength to climb the mountain. I wasn't anywhere near her, but found out later that Cebe had been far below urging her on.

We arrived at Camp Muir at 10,000 feet, and broke out above the clouds. From Paradise to our high camp at Camp Muir, we'd traveled uphill for six and a half hours. I felt as though I'd walked out of a dark theater into stark daylight and blinked like mad as I adjusted to the bright sunshine. The change lifted my spirits, with white clouds below, and sparkling snow that met the cloudless blue sky. It was gorgeous.

About a dozen tents were already set up. The place was a zoo. The buzz of conversations came from the climbers all around us. We'd taken the Disappointment Cleaver, or DC route and that's the most popular way up Mt. Rainier. Coupled with the fact that the good weather in July makes it a great time to do this climb, it was busy and getting busier. There was an almost festive atmosphere up there.

I investigated a shelter near the outhouse, where some people could sleep on wide shelves in a cramped little building. When I looked inside, the place was packed, and jeez did it stink! As miserable as the shelter was, the toilet was worse. It made me feel nauseous, so I opted out and peed in the snow.

When Jenny finally arrived, she was a wan, listless version of her former self. "Paula, I barely made it, and my head feels like it's about to split wide open." She slumped down on her sit pad. I was overheated from carrying my heavy pack for hours on end and was a little sweaty, but basically felt fine. "I'll set up our tent while you rest and make water for dinner." I didn't know anything about altitude sickness then, but I'd soon learn, since Jenny had the symptoms.

I got out my snow shovel and made a platform for our tent. There were no hotels to be found there and usually no flat places to pitch a tent either. Just as I finished my platform, Frank came over.

"You can't pitch your tent here."

"Why not? Looks like a good spot to me."

"This is not a good spot. It's not sheltered from the wind and if a storm blows in, it could blow your tent away."

"Not while I'm in it." Frank's face contorted and he began to shout at me.

"I'm telling you that you can't be here. Pick up your gear and move over there." He pointed to a spot next to his tent.

I shouted right back, "I'm not going to budge!" Frank was mad and who knows what he might've said next, when Cebe showed up and said my tent platform was in an acceptable position. Making a tent platform in packed snow is real work, and I thought, "What an ass! Who the hell does he think he is?"

Once the tent was set up Jenny climbed in, and I started melting snow to make hot water. I inhaled a freeze dried *Mountain House* meal intended for two. The directions said to wait a few minutes while the dehydrated shrimp puffed up, but I couldn't wait and kept fishing in the pouch with my spoon. I ended up eating partly crunchy shrimp and pasta for dinner. I hadn't felt hungry at all, until I smelled hot food, then realized that I was famished.

Soon as I finished eating, I stood outside the tent to brush and floss chunks of hard pasta out of my teeth. It was almost time to call it a day. The good news after we ate was that Jenny wasn't suffering, because she was out like a light. Cebe said when people have altitude sickness it normally took more than one night of sleep to adapt to high altitude, so I knew she wouldn't be going any further. After dreaming of doing this climb for years, she wasn't going to make it and I bet that hurt worse than her headache.

Most of the time, if someone gets altitude sickness, the best cure is to send them right back down the mountain, but no one in our group could accompany her down. We were all raring to go up, and anyone who wanted to head down would have to wait till we returned from the summit.

We were lucky to be doing this trip with experienced climbers like Cebe and Frank, even though I didn't like Frank anymore. No paid guides were needed, and our climb was a speedy two day trip. Most guided climbs on Mt. Rainier take three-and-a-half days. Lots of people shelled out big money when they used a guide service to make it to the top of this famous peak.

From high camp, we'd wait for several hours and start up in the middle of the night. The waiting interval was a good time to recuperate from climbing we'd done earlier that day. Our summit bid would take six–eight hours each way from Camp Muir, and we hoped to begin the ascent around midnight. At that time, the snow would be firm and less likely to avalanche. In summer, the sky stays light until 10pm in the Pacific Northwest. That made it almost impossible for me to sleep in the early evening.

Sleeping was out of the question for me, but not because it was light outside. I was too wound up, and kept peeking out of the tent. Once it got dark and I got an eyeful of the star-studded sky, I slipped outside.

Overhead the black sky was pierced with countless points of light. My mind drifted and the stars turned into thousands of fireflies, near our farm. On summer evenings, I walked down Mt. Falls Route to a bank of low, creamy fog at waist level. Tiny dots of light dipped in and out of it. When I heard a car coming, I stepped back to see the swirling mist part, as a car whooshed past me, and those lovely bugs splattered all over the windshield. I felt a firefly on my face and wiped it off, then realized I was wicked cold with snot dripping from my nose. I'd been dozing, and had to get some rest, so I got back into my sleeping bag. The most difficult part of the journey was about to begin.

After what seemed like an eternity, the time had arrived to dress for success, and luckily I'd caught a few z's. Jenny was still sick, and went back to sleep. Honestly, I didn't give her much thought, because at that point all I had on my mind was the summit. Since the majority of us had no idea what the hell we were doing, it took us a long time to get our act together.

My crampons were brand new; I'd neglected to try them on and couldn't figure out how they fit on my boots. Crampons look like metal teeth that fit on the bottom of climbing boots and allow for good purchase on ice. Fortunately, Cebe was checking each member of our party for readiness. I felt like an idiot as I struggled with the crampons, and he stopped to check me out. "Let me help you with that. Oh, these are new." Climbing gear is expensive, so most novices rent it. I was a novice, but I'd also decided this would not be my last alpine climb.

"I hope they get me to the top."

"Well, you have a good brand and they'll help on the ice."

"Hey, we're wearing the same gaiters!"

"All right. Your crampons are secure, and I've got to move on." He was leading our party of eight people and five of us were novices.

Everyone was ready to go, and we all did absolutely nothing! We waited, and waited and waited some more. Initially everyone was anxious and chatted away, but after a while that chatter ceased. The bitter cold was unsettling, and I did a little jig to help keep me warm. Climbers kept walking on by us as they began their ascent. I wondered what the hell was going on, and why they were going ahead of us. Finally I asked Cebe why we kept waiting. He said it was a common courtesy to allow R.M.I (Rainier Mountaineering Inc.) to take all their groups up first. I thought that sounded incredibly stupid. They weren't doing anything for us, so why were they so special? But, like the captain of a ship, Cebe was in charge, so I kept my mouth shut.

Cebe had to tie me into the rope, because I didn't have the faintest idea how to tie in, but since four other people were also being tied in, I supposed they felt as incompetent as me. The whole process of getting ready drove me nuts! There was no moon that night, so I was tied in and felt tied up, in below freezing temperatures in the pitch dark. Negative thoughts crept into my mind like, "I could've slept for at least another hour in my warm sleeping bag."

When I was just about to lose it, the rope team started to move. At last, we were all headed up to the top. In my imagination this all seemed so easy, because we'd just hike up snowfields to the summit then take pictures, see other mountains, and take an easy hike back down to the parking lot. Someone should've given me a reality injection.

All the while we'd waited to begin, I was like a horse chomping at the bit and pawing the ground. I couldn't wait to get out of the gate, but had no idea of what I was getting into. Climbing to the top of a mountain over 14,000 feet high actually involved a whole lot more than I'd ever imagined.

Even with a headlamp on, I couldn't see squat and since my visibility was nil, I assumed that was the reason we were going so slow. I figured we'd pick up the pace when it got light. Our only real training had been a rudimentary class on ice axe arrest, which taught us to shout "falling" and attempt to plunge our axe into the snow to stop. That's a technique which we could use if we were falling or if someone else on our rope team was falling into a crevasse. I didn't expect either of those things to happen, but you never know, and at least we were prepared.

I knew people died on Mt. Rainier. I'd scanned newspaper articles about that, but never read them in detail. Later I learned about the variety and extent of the circumstances that ended people's lives on The Mountain. Local people don't call it Mt. Rainier, but "The Mountain," as if there were no other. I'd heard stories on the news about bodies being recovered, and avalanches that buried people alive, but attributed that to bad luck and some bad mistakes. Of course, there's actually a lot more to it than that.

The unstable terrain on Mt. Rainier is largely responsible for the deaths that occur there every year. Snow, rock and ice falling down the mountainside can injure or kill anyone in its path. A climber trudging up the glacier can be swallowed whole without warning while plunging through the snow into a yawning chasm of ice. Even experienced leaders can lose their bearings in the dark and suddenly the entire party is lost. The weather is very unpredictable and it's possible to get caught in a bad storm without warning and freeze to death. Moving up a snow slope or plunge stepping down it, if the snow moves with you it's a big clue, as an avalanche buries you alive. Sometimes without any kind of warning, an avalanche swallows entire climbing parties.

Cebe mentioned something about crevasses once, but with no emphasis on how dangerous they could be. Many people who live near Seattle think climbing Rainier is just a hike up. Some of those people head up in sneakers and shorts and can end up paying for that hike with their lives, as they walk in this dangerous terrain, unprepared for a myriad of possible consequences.

Feeling cold became a distant memory, even though our progress was slow as molasses. The sky seemed closer to me as I climbed higher. With no buildings, trees or anything in sight, I was embraced by a black velvet heaven. To my left was the mountain and everything else was sky. Maybe it was the altitude, but I would've sworn that the sky expanded and I became incredibly small in turn. Everything that I saw was slightly illuminated by a soft, blue glow. I could just make out the strings of tiny lights that were the headlamps on climbers up ahead. On the rocks, we coiled up our ropes and used our ice axes to pick through boulders, rocks and scree. The metal crampons on our boots threw occasional sparks in the inky night, and sounded like fingernails on a chalkboard as we scraped and scratched the rocks.

At the Ingraham Flat, we were greeted by broken blocks of ice that had fallen sometime before from the glacier above. On the flat I saw huge chunks of ice the size of refrigerators and other chunks the size of small cars. The whole area was littered with shattered blocks of ice that had cleaved from the glacier. As we moved across that eerie place each one of us was quiet as a mouse. At dinner, a few hours before, someone told the story of the eleven people who'd been crushed to death by falling ice there.

We climbed up to the steepest part of the route: the snow and ice covered rock mass of Disappointment Cleaver. We'd already jumped over three crevasses, but it was so dark I hadn't been able to see down into them. Struggling up the Cleaver was the last time I touched solid ground. The rest of the way was pure snow and ice, until we reached the rocky crater rim on the summit.

We stopped at the top of the Cleaver to watch the spectacle of sunrise. Intense shades of magenta, flaming orange, and gold painted the morning sky with florescence and streaked through the horizon below us. Mt. Adams put on a show as she slipped into a shimmering pink veil of light. Daybreak on Rainier surpassed any dawn I'd ever witnessed. Even the gorgeous sunsets at sea level paled in comparison. It was a rare moment and I was lucky to be there. I'd read that native people believed Mt. Rainier was a sacred place, and thought the souls of their ancestors dwelled there. At that moment, I was a part of a world bathed in the astonishing beauty of the rising sun and it looked like heaven to me.

While we rested there, the skyline changed from a showcase of brilliant colors to the subtle, faded pastels I was more familiar with. We trudged straight up from there, and I saw climbers far ahead of us. The surface all around was textured and appeared to be thousands of tiny white mountains that stretched as far as the eye could see. Those little mountains were all fairly uniform in size and shape, and appeared to form the largest egg carton on earth.

In the light of day, I was disappointed that the pace didn't pick up. The next time we took a rest, Cebe coiled his rope and came back to talk to me and the others in our group. There was a long length of rope between each of us, so the only time we could talk to each other was when we stopped. Cebe asked me how I felt.

"I'm doing okay. Do you know why the snow looks like little mountains?"

"Oh, you mean the sun cups. They're formed when snow melts at high altitude."

"I've never seen anything like that before. It's funny looking. Oh, is there a reason we're going so slow?"

"For some people in our party this pace is just right, and we need to stay together. What did you think of the sunrise?"

"I was impressed. It's so colorful up here."

"It's really something isn't it? This slope is going to be tough going at some point, and when it is I use slow, deep breaths."

"Oh, you mean like combat breathing?"

"What's that?"

"In the Army I learned to do a count in between deep breaths. I didn't know breathing would be hard to do up here. If I feel out of breath, I'll try doing deep breathing. Right now I feel great!"

Cebe patted me on the back and checked on the other members of our rope team. After that rest we continued moving skyward. Somewhere, on the way up, we slowed even more. I looked up and saw Cebe take a step, pause for a second or two and then take the next step. I noticed I was gulping freezing air, and focused on slowing my breath. I inhaled through my nose and counted the seconds between each step. Cebe's tip about breathing helped me conserve energy, so I felt more relaxed on that long, last stretch to the top.

At 13,000 feet Clay and Dinah felt sick. Cebe and Frank got them into sleeping bags. They'd wait there and we'd help them on our way back down. I think they'd eaten something that made them feel bad. I learned later that the whole climb was put together for Clay.

Going up the last thousand feet, I focused on breath and put one boot in front of the other. It was brutally cold and the only thing that made it tolerable was the three layers of warm clothing between me and the frigid air. The temperature had me a little worried, but I knew I'd get to the summit, and get my picture taken.

# VICTORY SALUTE

IIIIIIIIIIIIIIIIIIIIIIIIIIIIIIIIIIIIIIIIIIIIIIIIIIIIIIIIIIIIIIIIIIIII

ONCE I WAS past the last bit of steep snow on the crater, I stood on the rocky rim of Mt. Rainier and looked down into the immense crater bed. Its size was impressive, and 30 feet below me was a flat snow-covered surface of unknown depth about 1,200 feet in diameter. Rainier has some hiccups now and then, but they're minor and she hasn't blown her top for thousands of years. No one can tell when, but someday she'll give an explosive repeat performance.

By the time we arrived at Columbia Crest at 14,410 feet — the highest point on Mt. Rainier — all of the professionally guided climbers were on their way back down the mountain. We signed the register, took group photos and were the only climbing party up there. Our group had been whittled down, and we ended up with Cebe, myself, Frank, his tent mate, and Gary. I asked who could take the photos of me, and Cebe said he had some skill with a camera, so I handed him mine.

The day before I'd clued everyone in about the plan for my summit picture, but only got mild reactions. So when Cebe shouted that he was ready to shoot, it was time for me to just do it! I yanked off my parka and the two layers below it, then undid my full side-zip pants, which left me in nothing but a thong and climbing boots. I used my pocketknife to cut off the thong and handed off my clothes and the knife. I dropped the thong on the snow, stepped on it so it wouldn't be visible, then grabbed my ice axe and held it over my head. I'd practiced that so many times in my apartment, timing myself, to be sure there wouldn't be a hitch in my performance. I did that in about two blinks of an eye, and not only was I high on a mountain top, but I was high on adrenaline.

Once I'd assumed my pose, Cebe started snapping pictures. The ice axe was sooo cold in my bare hands that it was hard for me to tell if the axe was freezing cold or burning hot. My face was numb, and just about every inch of my body reacted to the shocking cold with feelings that ranged from tingling to burning pain, and the gusting wind was an assault. Who knows what the wind chill was, but I know from personal experience it was torture. Those moments seemed incredibly long, and I was about to panic when Cebe shouted he'd gotten the pictures.

While I was literally freezing in the nude, I saw two men about a hundred yards away that were running toward me! I bet those two got splitting headaches from running at that altitude. I doubt those guys were on a heroic rescue mission, but since they never arrived while I was there I don't know what their story was.

My hands were completely numb. I couldn't feel my zippers, buttons, snaps or really anything at all, and I'm pretty sure I was becoming hypothermic. My friends had trouble figuring out the zippers on my pants, because just like a baby I had to be dressed by others. It seemed like it took them forever to get my clothes on, and all I remembered was having to stand still while they struggled with my outerwear.

Once dressed, I was cold as a popsicle and warmed my hands at the steam vents just below the summit. After my hands got some sensation back in them, I took an interest in things around me on Rainier that I hadn't noticed during the photo shoot. Hot air from the vents bloomed into wispy, white plumes and reminded me that "She's alive!" The frost didn't behave normally, and extended horizontally in lacy webs from the volcanic rocks. I didn't remember seeing Seattle, so I searched for a view of the city, but it was obscured in the haze below.

The steam vents had warmed my hands, but it took a while for the rest of me to thaw out. Our descent in the late morning sun felt good, but the top layer of the snowpack was melting. Slush balled up between my boots and crampons, and created the unpleasant sensation of a wad of newspaper stuck to the bottom of my boots. Whenever someone needed a rest, I spent the whole time trying to scrape that snow out. We collected the two sick climbers and continued down through the mush.

As we crept down from the summit, around about Cathedral Rocks I didn't think it was possible to go any slower, but we did. We were in a slow motion movie, with everyone picking their way down as though they'd lost something valuable on the way up. The thinning veneer that contained my emotions cracked and I started to silently cry. All I wanted was to get down to our camp, pack up, and leave. No one else on that damn rope team seemed to care what the hell was going on, as they dragged down the mountainside like zombies. Cebe was checking our progress and calmed me down with the assurance that we'd be at high camp soon.

In the light of day I finally had a good view of one of mother nature's finest creations. They were so impressive that I was really struck by them, and I took a few pictures of crevasses with my 35 mm camera. Later, when I got that film developed, those photos resembled bluish cracks in white mud, but in reality crevasses are some of the most beautiful things on earth.

Looking down into a wide crevasse where a glacier was riven open, it can appear to be endlessly deep. To me it looked like the largest glass sculpture on earth, with cool colors in shades of pale blue and white to deep aqua. In broad daylight, the crevasses made me think of Dale

Chihuly, our famous glass artist in Seattle. He really ought to go up the mountain in a helicopter and come down in a basket to get an eyeful, because no photo could ever capture the sheer beauty of that ice. Each was unique in depth and width, and after seeing them I began to appreciate how vast the glaciers on Mt. Rainier really are.

On the way down to high camp the stark landscape gave me the feeling that I was visiting another planet. There was nothing man-made there, and the white snow looked boundless, as it curved on the mountain and vanished against the sky. Growing up in the Northern Virginia countryside, I'd seen many deep winter snows, but nothing I'd ever seen before compared to the enormity of this place.

When we got down to high camp, Jenny was up and moving around. She felt a little better and was ready to go home. I packed up the tent after we fixed a meal, and we were ready to leave. Frank's partner came over.

"Paula, do you remember Frank and me dressing you?"

"Ummm, yes." I nodded.

"We were wondering if you also remember what you said to us." Her eyes narrowed.

"Uh...no, was I talking to you?" I was beginning to feel worried.

"I can't say that I'd call it *talking* to me, but you sure talked all right."

"What-what did I say?" My worry was turning to fear.

"What the fuck is taking you so long? You've seen everything. Can't you just get these damn pants on me?"

Once I heard those words, the F bomb echoed in my head and I knew I'd said that. I was embarrassed, and mumbled something about being colder than fuck. Cursing my helpers might've been an example of my impatience, as I waited to be dressed, or a response triggered by my survival instinct. Either way, I don't think I ever thanked them properly, and they'd literally saved my ass.

That morning we'd climbed up over 4,000 feet and by the time we reached Paradise would have descended another 10,000. Once I'd packed up and was on my way down, I experienced either one of the after-effects of a huge adrenaline surge or a side effect of hypothermia and exhaustion, or maybe even a combo of the two. My legs turned to jelly, and I must have looked like I was doing a comic stunt, because I kept stumbling and falling over like a drunk. Gary offered me one of his ski poles, and it was a lifeline for me. I don't think I could've made it down to the parking lot without it. By the time we got to the cars, it was dark, and since Jenny was rested she drove us home.

My summit pictures turned out perfect. For some reason Cebe took pictures of me from almost every angle including the front. I got the film developed by Nick Felkey, the best photographer on the island. I had an idea, and asked our postmaster if I could send a nude photo in the mail as a postcard. He said yes, as long as there was no frontal nudity. I had a good butt shot and decided to make 100 copies and send them to all my friends, clients and family as Christmas postcards. I became something of a celebrity at our post office after that.

On the summit, I barely knew anyone — no pun intended. The weirdest part of that photo shoot was that I only remember the extreme cold and wind, but had no thoughts of being self-conscious at all! The undress rehearsals I'd done at home helped me play my part in the little movie in my head.

Climbing Mt. Rainier is difficult and exhausting. It can be dangerous, and is shockingly cold. Getting naked on top of that mountain was no small feat, and I'm the only person who's ever done it. You might say 'of course you're the only one who has done that, because it's a crazy thing to do.' I'd counter that with; believe it or not, that was a calculated and well-planned event.

The Nike swoosh on my buzz cut is barely discernible, but it's there.

Most people who gave me feedback on that photo thought it was an audacious stunt, and one recipient suggested I sell the pictures to a professional photographer on Bainbridge Island. No one seemed to get the point of it at all!

Originally, I'd wanted a photo that illustrated my ability to give up everything to reach the summit of Mt. Rainier. But I was surprised to see something quite different. I'd become androgynous, stripped of the vestiges of femininity, and powerfully bold in my victory salute. I thought about selling those pictures for maybe a whole minute, but they're priceless to me. One person who should've gotten one of those photos, but didn't, was Marsha. I had no way to get in touch with her, but she would've known instantly what that picture was about.

# ISLAND FRIENDS AND A
# SHOT OF MT. SHUKSAN

||||||||||||||||||||||||||||||||||||||||||||||||||||||||||||||||||||||||||||||||||||||||||||

AS A PERSONAL trainer, I spent a lot of time in the gym working for other people, and looked forward to my own workouts a couple times a week. I did a maintenance routine, unless Marsha showed up. When she was in the gym, my workout turned into an interesting collaboration with her.

Marsha was a Seattle firefighter, and I suspected she could kick most men's asses. I loved to work out with her, because she was one of the few women who could spot me and lift heavier than I did. With a strong personality and a good sense of humor, she enlivened my day. Attractive and built to last, what an incredibly powerful woman she was. We weren't power lifters or bodybuilders, but shared a love of strength training. We couldn't make a plan to meet, because our schedules conflicted, so I was always tickled whenever she just happened to be in the gym at the same time as me. Eventually she disappeared, and I didn't know if she moved or what happened to her. I missed our workouts together, but most importantly I missed her friendship.

My ability to develop and maintain friendships needed an overhaul. Many people viewed me as a sportswoman who was a hard ass. Most of my clients had sought me out because they needed someone to crack the whip. That demeanor was helpful at work, but it wasn't the real me. My carefully crafted disguise concealed that I was self-conscious. Being shy was an unfortunate personality trait and a big stumbling block that I still wrestle with.

I appeared to be a buoyant, brusque and self-possessed woman who rushed around the gym like a lioness in search of prey. So when a quiet elderly man introduced himself to me at the gym, I'm sure he sensed I wasn't all that. Richard was soft-spoken with short, white curls and a lean build. I'd noticed him before when he was working out on machines in the gym, and we'd exchanged smiles. He asked me if he could touch my hair and I said, "Go ahead." He lightly ran his hand over my silky buzz and gave me such a genuine smile of pleasure that I had to smile in return. I didn't know him, but recognized something we had in common. He had a trait that I had in spades — aloneness. I didn't know if he could tell I was a kindred spirit, but I was.

While my hair was short, every time he crossed my path on the street or in a store, no matter who was there and even in the company of a friend, I'd walk right up to him and wordlessly bow my head. I didn't care what anyone else might think. I'm sure our strange ritual must've caused some pause for thought, but it was such a small thing to do and it made him so happy.

With no close friends to confide in, my dad was one of two people I'd talk to about serious matters. I was often afraid I'd upset him and couldn't talk to my step-mom either, because she'd be sure to share it with him. As luck would have it, a new friendship was about to form.

Jake and I hit it off right away on a hike in the Olympic Mountains, and afterward we continued to hike and climb together. When we went up steep switchbacks, he told jokes and seemed so carefree. I'd never met anyone quite like him, because he was so comfortable in the middle of nowhere, as if he'd always been there. He was tall and had a medium build tending towards heavy, but was nimble. I think his best feature was his shoulder-length wavy blond hair that was streaked with gray. When we talked about my climb on Mt. Rainier, he laughed at the description I gave him of my summit picture. He shared some of his climbing experiences with me, and I learned he was a very good mountaineer and rock climber.

When he invited me to climb Mt. Shuksan, I was jazzed and could barely contain my excitement. I jumped at the invitation because I couldn't wait to do my third alpine climb. I learned later that Shuksan is the most photographed mountain in the Cascades. Its jagged peak lit with pink alpenglow graces postcards and wall calendars. It was beautiful, but for me it wasn't the mountain's appearance that was the most impressive thing about it.

I met up with Jake and the rest of the guys in the climbing party at the pub on the Island to plan the climb on Shuksan. My hair was growing out but was very short, and I'd dyed it dark auburn. Everybody got a pint of beer and we talked about the climb. That afternoon the restaurant filled up with noisy people. Jake spread a topographical map out on the table, and we all peered at it during the conversation about the logistics of the trip. I didn't have much to say, but thought planning the trip was very interesting, since I'd never been in on that stage of a climb before.

I thought all those guys would make great climbing companions, with one exception. We all had some doubts about Jay. He admitted he had no glacier experience, and would be wearing brand new boots on the trip. Jay assured us he'd get them broken in. I hoped he would wear those new boots night and day, because he didn't have much time to break them in. With some climbing experience, and after being vetted by another climber in our group, he was in. That meeting took an hour or so then we set a date to go.

The night before that trip, my neighbor Jean knocked at my door.

She lived below me, in the Quay Apartments and was about 15 feet above the parking lot. She'd locked herself out and wondered if my key might open her door. It didn't, and she was upset because her daughter was on her way there, and Jean needed to fix her dinner.

I asked if she kept the sliding glass doors locked on her balcony, because I didn't lock mine. She said no, and then I knew what to do. I told her I'd rappel onto her balcony and walk through the apartment to open the front door. She was thrilled with my suggestion. I'd practiced rappelling from my balcony before and knew I could do it.

She'd called the property manager's office, but it wasn't open so she could only leave a message. The only other way for her to get in would be to call a locksmith and they cost a bundle. I dug my harness out of my backpack, got an ATC (a device to help control the rope) and a used climbing rope that I'd been given. I rappelled onto her deck and had her back in her home lickety-split. It only took me a few minutes to help, and was no skin off my nose. I rarely saw her during the 6 years I lived there, and I think that was the first and last time we spoke.

I got up early the next morning and drove to Jay's house to carpool with him and Joe. For some strange reason, Joe decided to stop at the grocery store on the way to the ferry. That bothered me, because I was ready to go, and this guy wasted about 30 minutes of our time, but we still made the 7:10 boat. It struck me that since I was climbing with Joe and Jay and would be joined by Jake, that I'd be climbing with the three Jays. I hoped they got along better than the blue jays at my bird feeder.

That day was cloudless as the sun came up. When we got to the boat, the horizon turned sherbet orange with some blue peeking through. Joe was jovial and easy on the eye, so I decided to try and forget about his shopping spree.

At first sight Shuksan got oohs and ahhs from us. Jay pulled the car over; we saw a climbing route called Fisher Chimneys and talked about possibly attempting that route in the future. I thought the granite that ran up the side of Shuksan looked like a stegosaurus's back.

The guys took a lot of pictures, but I'd gotten into the lazy habit of collecting postcards, instead of taking pictures. When I was stationed in Europe with the military police, I didn't have a camera and postcards served my need for images. My postcard collection included a good picture of Mt. Shuksan, so that day I didn't take any.

Right after Sandy and Dean met us at the trailhead, Joe sat right down on the ground and stuffed his face. As he ate, the rest of us milled around, and I was pissed. Imagine that! Obviously, he hadn't prepared well, but I'd gotten up at 4:30 in the morning, fixed oatmeal and a big pot of coffee. I'd brought freeze dried meals, and I'd bought them months before. Being prepared is important, so I was almost fit to be tied as I watched him pig-out, while me and the other guys were ready to go. I wanted to walk right over and kick his shit all over the place.

I'd brought my tent, but since my Swedish stove was heavy, I got to use Jay's. To make up for carrying less gear, I volunteered to carry pickets (used as anchors in the snow), tent poles, and other metal objects. No one questioned my ability, but as the smallest member of the party and the only woman in it, I wanted to show them that I wasn't a weakling.

Jake had told us at the meeting he'd be sleeping in late on the morning of the climb, and we knew we'd see him sooner or later, so we started up without him. The trailhead was easy to find, but it was a long trip up to our high camp, and none of us had taken that trail before. We hoped we'd have no trouble following it, and figured Jake would catch up with us along the way.

Over an hour went by before we needed to check the map. That October in the woods was a scenic hike up. The colorful trees low on the trail thinned and the woods gradually became a thick pine forest that opened periodically to give us glimpses of Mt. Baker. When we got into the most dense part of the forest we had trouble figuring out which way to go. There were no visible landmarks and we wondered if we'd gone the wrong way.

Dean and Joe looked at the map again and used a compass as Jay doctored his blisters. We had walkie talkies, but hadn't heard from Jake. About then, the trail completely vanished and then it was a hop, skip and jump over downed trees. At last Jake contacted us. His handle was Show Buff, Jay was Lucky Man and Dean was Devil Mouse. Jay and Dean checked in with Jake periodically to monitor his progress, and got tips on the terrain. Those code names made for some silly conversations.

After confirming that we were going the right way, we took a lunch break, and ate on a small flat spot under some pine trees. A big clump of wet snow dropped on my peanut butter sandwich and turned it into mush, and another went down the back of my neck. Other than chilly wet snow melting under my shirt, I felt good in only one layer of clothing. The weather forecast was for temps in the low sixties, but at 4,000 feet it wasn't that warm. We were close to the snow line, and I felt good, mainly because we were in the sun and almost constantly moving.

We got to an old clear cut, with very small trees beginning to poke up above the stumps and saw Mt. Baker. She jumped right up in front of us, and seemed to be a bit of a showoff that day as she fairly glowed and was sporting an intricate lacy look. I saw huge fissures (crevasses) that created that pattern all over her. We all felt pretty good except for Jay and by then he was hobbling up the mountain. We didn't stop there, and kept moving up.

Sandy was slender and taller than me. From then on, he and I led the way. We were light and fast like a couple of little Sherpas, and talked about our love of running. The heavier guys disappeared behind us, as we cruised on up. I guess the upside of being small is that we traveled light and fast.

We ran into a hunter and exchanged greetings. I was glad he hadn't mistaken Sandy or me for a deer, but thought if he had shot me by mistake that I would've looked pretty good next to his other trophies. We hiked up an open ridge with more fabulous views of Mt. Baker to the left and Baker Lake to the right. It got really steep on the scramble up a bank of rock and wet snow. That was the most difficult part of the climb for me, and I had to use my hands. I hadn't bothered to get gloves out of my pack and in no time my hands were ice cold. More than once I teetered as I tried to regain my balance. Sandy was just above me and he didn't falter at all. At one hundred twenty-five pounds with a pack that weighed over fifty, that rocky bit was a struggle for me.

As I wobbled on that snowy bank, I thought about my horse Zack and wondered if he'd ever felt like this when I was on his back. Still, that rocky ridge was a short distance to go, and once I made it to the top, I got my gloves on. There were only a few trees at the top of the ledge, and after we passed that spot I wouldn't see another tree until we came back down.

At about 3:30 in the afternoon, Sandy and I stood at the top of that rocky bank of snow and saw the col (a col looks like the curved part of a horse's saddle). That was an important landmark for us, because then we knew we were close to the high camp. I felt chilled and dug out a fleece jacket and my parka. At that time of year, the sun would be going down around six, but we were in no hurry and waited for the others to join us. From where we stood, we had a gorgeous view of Baker Lake sparkling below.

Sandy and I headed up when we saw the rest of the guys. The col was a huge, concave, almost vertical snowfield. The other men could see us and follow up. It was so steep there that I thought we might use pickets, but we managed to climb to high camp without them.

We crossed talus, a field of loose rock, that was part of the drainage from the glacier. Then we climbed the steep snow slope, and I could see two other climbers above us setting up their camp. Sandy and I waved as we passed them, and about two hundred yards from there, we waited for the others to join us. The nearby mountains were green with pines and further away turned to blue in the distance. Pure, pristine snow with no footprints but our own draped the whole mountain from where we stood. That spot jutted out just at the snout of the glacier and I could see far into the valley below.

There was a toilet with no walls — just a commode below our camp that faced out to the valley. When I had to go pee, I nearly hopped off the pot, because I heard what sounded like a massive car wreck far below me. Jake explained to me later that what I'd heard was the sound of glacial ice as it crashed down the side of the mountain. We could all hear it on and off throughout the time we were in the campsite. Years before, I'd crossed Coastal Highway 1 to walk to the beach in Morro Bay, when I saw two cars collide near me. That sound was similar to the ice fall, except this sounded more muffled, went on and on, and was much more thunderous than a car wreck, as massive hunks of glacial ice cleaved and shattered below.

After we'd all pitched our tents and had dinner, the three J's were posturing and joking around with Sandy and Dean. Most of them were old friends who'd climbed together before. Jake was the only one I knew, and he didn't seek my company. There was way too much testosterone in the air, so I climbed into my tent. It seems ironical now that I spent that evening snuggled up with Ernest Hemingway's *The Sun Also Rises*.

That night, in my dream, the eerie sound of the ice falls morphed into plates and glasses that smashed on the tiled kitchen floor. I ran to my sister's crib and felt like I was running on Jell-O. She was crying and shaking like a leaf. My family wasn't hurt, but water had sloshed out of the pool and everything in the house was topsy turvy. That was a dream about the earthquake that caused my family to flee California and seek refuge in Virginia. The rest of my dreams that night were peopled with my family members.

At five in the morning, I popped out of my tent fully dressed and ready to go. We were covered by a dense cloud of fog. I could barely see the tent next to me, and picked my way over to Jake's bivy sack. I woke him up and learned never to wake Jake. I asked when we'd go and like a turtle he stuck his head out of his bivy. He was grumpy and gruffly informed me that we'd wait an hour or so. We sure did wait, and started up three and a half hours later! The fog was long gone and it was warming up.

Jake said that if the conditions were good we might be able to summit. I was roped to him and Sandy. None of us had ever been on that mountain before, so in addition to being a climb it was an adventure. We headed up to a ridge that a bank of fog still clung to. As the fog evaporated it looked like someone was tearing off pieces of cotton candy and tossing them into the wind as they dissolved. Jake pointed out Lake Ann far below and Mt. Baker appeared to be just a stone's throw away.

We moved along the ridge, and then from a distance saw the summit. There was no question about it, and I'll never forget it, because it looked so strange. I'd compare it to a giant size, upside down vanilla ice cream cone liberally sprinkled with nuts and dashes of creamy snow. That odd summit block looked as if it had been dropped there by accident. The closer we got to it, we saw snow pouring off that pile of jagged boulders that led to the top. There was way more than dashes of snow on it.

We ascended, and only got about halfway up, when all of us were pretty sick and tired of being dumped on by small avalanches of snow. The men decided to turn back in favor of safety. I only wished we'd headed to the top when I'd wanted to. Some of the guys whipped out cameras and took photos on the summit block. The bird's eye view of Mt. Baker was so unique that I took a couple, but my pictures had someone's head in them.

There's not much to say about our descent except that Jay's blisters were awful, and the most horrible ones I'd ever seen. I would have sworn a small animal had gnawed on his bloody feet. I gave him most of my moleskin donuts to reduce the friction from his new boots, but with feet like that there's no practical way to make them feel better short of amputation. Jay hiked gingerly, but was a good sport and nary a peep escaped his lips.

Even though we didn't reach our goal, that was one of the best climbs I've ever done, for two reasons. To say that Shuksan is picturesque is an understatement; she's gorgeous, but what impressed me the most were the explosive sounds of the ice falls.

Jake and I talked a bit as we got all of our equipment sorted out and packed into the cars. He said he was a member of a wilderness club and was going to lead a hike up Mt. Ellinor. He wondered if I wanted to go. I told him I'd love to. Then I asked him if I needed to join the club. He said, "No, you'll be my guest, but you might want to join after you learn more about the club and meet some of the members."

When I'd finished *The Sun Also Rises*, it was the first book that I'd read by Ernest Hemingway, and wondered why I hadn't read his work before. I just loved it. Years later, after having read all of his books, I decided to find out if he was known for any famous quotes. He is quoted on several subjects, but I was wowed when I discovered this one: "There are only three sports: bullfighting, motor racing, and mountaineering; all the rest are merely games."

# ROCK 101 AND A CHANCE MEETING

ON THE HIKE that Jake led up Mt. Ellinor, I met a man named Shakti. We got to know each other as we ascended up through the forest. That trail was challenging at times, but like a fine wine had a beautiful finish. He told me rock climbing was his latest passion and that he practiced at an indoor climbing gym. Then he invited me to climb with him there.

His perfect smile, shiny black hair and golden brown skin piqued my interest, but I thought rock climbing was pretty damn scary. I told him I'd need to think about it, since I didn't have any experience and was a big chicken. He laughed and said that he wasn't great at it, but could teach me the basics.

The very idea of climbing hand over fist straight up a rock wall had no more appeal to me than taking part in an accident waiting to happen. Alpine climbing in mountain boots with an axe was tough. But rock climbing? At my age? I'd look like a climbing grandma compared to youngsters in their teens and twenties. On the way up the trail I mulled it over. Many mountains had features that required rock climbing, and if I picked up that skill I'd be a better mountaineer. I told Shakti I'd like to give it a try, and we made a date to meet at Stone Gardens in Seattle. I asked if I needed to buy any equipment, and he told me I could rent it there.

Stone Gardens brought the reality of my advanced age into sharp focus. The place was full of children from age seven on up. Shakti gave me a lesson on how to belay (belay means managing the rope for the climber), and we scouted for an easy route. The walls were covered with man-made hand holds and weren't inviting, because I thought they might pop right off at any moment. Those holds were brightly colored blobs resembling Play-Doh and angular objects that were attached to gray walls. Shakti went up with ease, and I thought I should be able to do that and did. We moved to another 5.6, and it was no problem, but when we got to the 5.7 it was tough for me. I thanked Shakti and decided to call it quits, but was catching on quickly and hoped to improve with practice.

As I headed to the door, I was pretty excited about that first try at rock climbing, until I saw small children outperforming me. A boy about ten-years-old flew up a route, as he quickly moved from one brightly colored bobble to the next ascending at lightning speed. That kid really stole my thunder because I thought I'd done well. I continued to scan the gym and saw a woman a little younger than me who climbed slowly and often glanced down until she popped off the wall and was lowered to safety. Clearly I was an oldster in that playground, but I knew I could get better at rock climbing and decided to stick with it.

I tried to find a friend to go to Stone Gardens with me, and one time I brought Jeanie. I'd met her and her husband Jason when I lived near them in the same neighborhood with my second husband. She had no rock climbing experience, and was a natural, but wasn't interested in doing it again. I'd lost touch with Shakti, and Jake didn't have time to go to Seattle. Without a partner, I didn't get a lot of experience, until Vertical World opened a new climbing gym about forty-five minutes from my apartment.

That rock gym was the only one in Kitsap County, and as far as I knew it was also the only one on the entire Olympic Peninsula. I was delighted when I heard about it, because it literally saved me a boatload of time. Before it opened, I had to take the ferry to Seattle and then drive to the gym. Now I was more than ready to try out the new place and by then I had rock shoes, a chalk bag, a belay device, and a good climbing harness and that was everything I needed to climb indoors. Well, that and a partner.

At Vertical World, I slowly, but surely, made progress. I often practiced on overhangs and traversing in the bouldering area. I didn't need a partner to do those moves. Traversing is something we did a lot in mountaineering and overhangs were always a good puzzle. I didn't want to dyno, (basically jumping to your next position on the route) but if my climbing partner encouraged me enough I'd try it. I hated to jump when I was up high.

Both sport climbing and traditional climbing are different versions of free climbing. Sport climbers clip into bolts at indoor gyms and at outdoor climbing areas. Traditional climbers don't need bolts to clip in to and carry their own traditional protection (trad pro). Trad pro is a collection of gear that can be placed in rock walls and then later removed. Eventually I'd become a fair trad climber who could comfortably climb routes rated 5.8 to 5.9.

Leaving Vertical World one evening, I saw a woman on the cover of a climbing magazine, and picked it up. I didn't read the whole story and bought the magazine. That article was about Lynn Hill who made the first free ascent of "The Nose" on El Capitan in Yosemite. A lot of men had tried to do that and failed. Lynn was the first person to complete that incredibly difficult climb. Then she came back the following year and did it in record time. She's one of the best climbers in the world bar none!

In my Nissan king cab, I studied the pictures of her. She was a pretty blonde and didn't look very tall. I'd always thought I was too short to be a good rock climber, but when I read she was only 5'2" I was inspired!

She was two inches shorter than me. I said to myself, Aretha Franklin is "The Queen of Soul," but Lynn Hill is truly "The Queen of Rock" and my hero. Instead of worrying about being short, I'd learned that my height wasn't necessarily a disadvantage. Creativity in route finding would be my guide. It was getting dark when I put that magazine down and went home.

As I drove along Highway 3, the cab of my truck filled with thick, black smoke that had a chemical smell. I coughed as I rolled the window down and thought it might be my old truck's last gasp. I managed to get off at the next exit, and then the truck died. I rolled downhill, steered onto the shoulder of the street, and parked completely off the road, but was in a no parking zone. I'd have to get the truck towed to my mechanic's shop.

I was dressed in tiny running shorts and a jog bra, because I hadn't planned to stop on the way home. I fumbled around behind my seat but didn't find a jacket or a sweater. It was around 9 p.m. by then, and I didn't have a cell phone, so I walked to the Circle K hugging myself in the cold night air and used a pay phone. After calling a couple of friends for help, I was awfully cold and couldn't get anyone to answer. I was in a fix and needed a ride, but didn't have a credit card with me and had to go home to get one and have my truck towed.

I hurried into the store and warmed my hands near a rotating rack of hotdogs. A young clerk asked me what was wrong. I must've looked pathetic and half frozen when I explained what happened. He said he'd get off work pretty soon and would give me a ride. I was surprised and thought he was either a good Samaritan or an axe murderer, but was in no position to judge his hobbies. He dropped me off at my apartment and asked if there was anything else he could do to help. I thought of a number of things he could do for me, but said, "No. Thanks a lot."

I ran upstairs, pulled a sweatshirt on, got the credit card, then called the tow truck company and described where my truck was. They said they'd be there in about 45 minutes. I hung up and instantly panicked. because I had no way to get there! I became a frenzied bimbo and went outside running around looking for apartments in my complex with lights on. My brilliant plan was to ask any neighbor who answered the door to give me a lift.

The lights were on in only one of the apartments, and I knocked steadily until a man answered the door. "Hi, I'm your neighbor and I live there" I said breathlessly pointing to my apartment. "My truck broke down in Poulsbo, and I have no way to get there and a tow truck is on the way!" I was a nervous wreck and hoped he didn't think I was a maniac. He glanced back into his apartment while I talked.

"My niece is here, and I don't want to leave her alone. What's your name?"

"Paula."

"I'm Chance, hang on a minute. I'll talk to her and see if I can help you." I hoped he'd give me a chance to get to my truck. He returned jingling keys in hand and said, "Okay, let's go."

We talked as he drove to my truck and I discovered that I liked him. Chance managed to get me there just in the nick of time. We followed the truck to my mechanic's shop and my new friend Chance took me home. He then got an open invite to stop by and have a cold one with me anytime. He smiled and said he'd take me up on that. The only thing wrong with my vehicle was a broken hose that was cheap to repair. Everything turned out fine after all, and I began to think about the merits of a cell phone and a good friend who would take my calls.

After the repair, she ran like a top. I only had two clients that I worked with in their homes, so I didn't drive it a lot and wondered if I should sell the truck and get a motorcycle. I decided to keep it because it might come in handy on some climbing trips.

I walked to the gym a few minutes away from my apartment to

workout, and planned to focus on my back. In the locker room one of my clients said hi. We chatted for a bit and she asked if I'd heard about Ken Cross. I hadn't thought about him recently, but had hiked with him. I learned that he'd walked into city hall with his chain saw running, because he was upset about all the trees being cut down for the new ballpark near his home. I asked if he'd been arrested and she wasn't sure.

I was amazed to hear that, because I'd spent some time with him and he'd seemed like a very reasonable man. Occasionally I made jokes about axe murders, but I'd never considered a potential chain saw massacre that involved Ken.

I put that news out of my mind and got on with my pull-ups. When I'd finished my last repetition someone behind me said, "Good work!" I jumped down, and saw Cebe. We talked about his workout, and I gave him a couple of tips.

We started to compare notes on our outdoor activities, and I bragged that I was climbing 5.8's. He was a little surprised and then invited me to do the real thing! He was going to rock climb at the Tooth on Snoqualmie Pass and asked me if I'd like to go. It's a classic class five, three plus pitch route (a pitch is as far as you can go on the length of your climbing rope). The main thing to know about class five is that you rope up after 5.4. How could I say no? All I'd done up until then was climb on fake rock under a roof.

Don't get me wrong, I think indoor climbing is a good thing. I learned a lot at indoor climbing gyms, and they come in handy when you can't climb outside. When Vertical World in Bremerton closed, I was sad to hear about that.

The morning we left the island to climb the Tooth, I was so excited that I got up in the pitch dark at 4 AM to get ready. My preferred morning nosh was always the same thing, old fashioned oatmeal with a dark

French roast coffee, which I always enjoyed. I was on top of the world, as I double-timed it to the ferry terminal in mountain boots with a pack.

Cebe and I met on the 5:30 AM boat, and he led me to an area on the ferry with rows of plastic chairs bolted to the floor. It was in the middle of the boat and I'd never sat there before because there wasn't much of a view. He informed me that this was where the climbers sat. I thought, "Huh, so sitting there is a signal that you're a climber." After that day, I always sat near there in hopes of meeting a potential climbing partner, and sometimes listened to climbers discussing their trips.

We set our packs on the floor and talked about the climb. "Have you hiked or climbed around Snoqualmie Pass before?"

"No I haven't, and I've only rock climbed indoors."

"You'll see what a great hiking area it is once we get there. We'll go partway on the trail then go off trail and scramble a bit. It's beautiful and draws a lot of hikers, but we're going in so early that we probably won't see anyone. On the way, we'll pass a couple of small lakes in the area and see one that looks more like a tarn." Not only did I not know what a tarn was, but even though I'd scrambled I wasn't familiar with that term yet. I was afraid he'd think I was dumb if I asked about those things, so I didn't. He asked me "Do you know how to rappel?"

"I've only practiced from my balcony."

"We have to rappel on the way down from the Tooth. You're in good shape and I don't think you'll have any trouble."

"How long have you been climbing?"

"About thirty years."

"Wow! You know I'm just getting the hang of it and so far I've only done three alpine climbs."

"That's a good start considering you just got into it this year. Since we live so close to two mountain ranges, you'll soon climb more mountains"

"What's your favorite alpine climb?"

"Mt. Constance. I try to get up there at least once a year with my buddy Lionel, and I think it's one of the most challenging and beautiful climbs in the Olympics."

"I think the shape of that mountain is pretty. Why is it so challenging?"

"It's tough going almost right away. Shortly after leaving the forest road, the trail becomes almost vertical and that's just the beginning of it." We continued to talk about rock and mountain climbing. I grabbed my pack and we got into his car as we docked in Seattle.

In the Alpental Ski Area that morning in late-September, the crisp air was filled with the musical sound of birds as we hiked up the trail. At Snow Lake, our path was covered with fiery stars that were elm leaves.

We scrambled over a huge bowl of loose, medium sized rocks called talus just above Source Lake. Fat furry pikas scurried and chirped nearby. Pikas are in the rabbit family, but are smaller and resemble hamsters on steroids. Those guys would suddenly pop up out of nowhere, take a look, and squeak out some message, probably "go away," then vanish. I'll admit I felt stupid for not bringing my camera, because I'd never seen pikas before. That was a day of firsts for me.

To our right we saw another good climb called "The Chair" and talked about possibly doing that. The rocky hillside led us past drifts of mountain heather blooming pink and sparkling under frost crystals. We looked up and spotted the Tooth towering above us. It was just past more talus and scree and looked nearby, but getting there was work.

Once past the rocky rubble, we braced ourselves against the walls of a steep gully, and pulled ourselves up about 200 feet. That was no task for the weary, and from there it was down, then around and back up to the starting point of our roped climb.

Since I'd never rappelled on rock, Cebe taught me the finer points. Also I'd never used traditional protection before. He showed me his set of metal cams and chunks of metal in different sizes and shapes and then taught me how the gear worked. After that, up we went!

An enormous raven flew by as we ascended. Cebe knew this rocky peak well and didn't need a route map, so we didn't waste any time trying to figure out moves. That was really a kick because we moved up smoothly without a hitch. That place put all the climbing gyms to shame, and after climbing there *all* I wanted to do was climb outdoors.

Near the top, I came to something called the Cat Walk. Little did I know that Cebe must've been really looking forward to that. He hadn't said word one about it. All of a sudden I was on a ledge three inches wide in big chunky boots, and the rough rock surface only offered some fingertip holds for balance.

Carefully working my way across that narrow ledge, I was balancing with a finger or two, and Cebe called "Look down, Paula." I bet he'd taken all the slack out of the rope, because the Cat Walk is the real McCoy. Crossing it is so far from using man-made handholds in a gym that there's no comparison and negotiating on that narrow ledge will undoubtedly make or break a rock climber. Since all I'd done was focus on climbing up, I hadn't bothered to look down and when I did I saw a sheer drop off that was hundreds of feet straight down. I was a rock climber to the core because my only reaction was one of pure elation. I was absolutely thrilled to be there and called up, "I love it!"

I was close to the summit then, and once there — boy — what a view! The trees were gorgeous, dressed in fall colors. Red vine maples, elms and hot orange huckleberry spread out below us. From there, as far as the eye could see, was a string of blue mountain peaks that vanished into the distance. The speed limit on Highway 90 was 60, and was so far below us that the tiny cars on it moved as slow as molasses.

After a feast of sushi, bagels, beef jerky and chocolate, we kicked back and rested. High above the madding crowd we watched a storm front magically materialize. Dark clouds and strong winds rushed us, so we grabbed our stuff and made a speedy retreat on our rappel down. Rappelling! Oh my god-how I loved that! Once down off the Tooth, we beat feet back to the car in the dark with headlamps.

Rain dumped on us, as we drove away and I poured my heart out. Cebe heard the saga of my last failed marriage. I'd firmly believed that my second husband, David, and I were a match made in heaven when we got married. If he'd been salt, I was pepper, and he balanced my quirky personality with his calm one.

What a kind man he was, who paid attention to the little things. He'd surprise me with the gift of something that I'd only picked up to admire. He once said that I was the perfect woman who was beautiful, loved baseball, and was just like one of the guys. That was a sincere compliment, but it took me a minute or two to understand, and I knew he was my knight in shining armor.

We lived together for a year before we got married, and by then my son Matt was eleven-years-old. David's home was in California, and we flew Matt down to join us for the summer. Matt hated it there as much as he'd hated Virginia. He ended up running away, and I sent him home right after that. Then I told David I needed to move back up to Washington and live closer to my sons.

Within just a few months, David found a new job in Seattle. We packed up and moved there, then Matt moved in and he hated it there too. I just couldn't seem to provide him with an environment he wanted to be in, so he went back to his dad's house again. David and I got married, and then decided to move to Bainbridge Island. We bought a big four-bedroom home on an acre of land, and I thought, maybe Willy, Max and Matt would all join us there someday.

I went to work as a mail carrier and struggled to deliver all the mail. Every day that I worked in the post office I felt overwhelmed and didn't know if I could ever deliver all the letters and packages. One night I was having a bad dream about filing all the letters correctly for delivery, and my husband woke me up, because I was filing mail into the headboard of our bed. At breakfast, he told me I should quit that job. He was right and I did.

David helped me start my own company, because he was sure I could find work in people's homes as a personal trainer. Even though the local gym was small, I worked with a few people there, and it didn't take long before I got busy. I didn't make a lot of money, but I could buy our groceries, clothes, and gifts for my kids.

When David lost his job about a year after we moved to the island, he turned into a different person. I couldn't talk to him without making him angry. We found a marriage counselor who said maybe we shouldn't be married, then promptly fired him and hired another. The new counselor didn't help either, and I think we would've tried almost anything to fix our marriage, but we didn't know what else to do. I started to think that I should just walk out.

The end came abruptly, and took us both by surprise. One morning David really rattled my cage. He told me we were running out of money and that he needed to know how much I made to help pay the bills. That was the straw that broke this camel's back. Mind you, we'd never co-mingled our funds, because when we married, he'd told me his mother was afraid I was after his money! Now he wanted me to hand over all my money, and I said, "I'm getting a divorce." It was a knee jerk reaction, and I really hadn't thought it through.

Cebe had been married for over 30 years, but listened patiently to my pathetic story. He gave me some good advice and wasn't judgmental. I asked him if I was hopeless or if he thought that someday I might find a good husband. He smiled and told me not to worry, because eventually I'd meet the right man. The value of our friendship went up considerably for me that night.

We talked about snowshoes after my gory divorce story, and Cebe told me what to look for when I shopped for a new pair. For some reason while he was giving me that advice I saw a parallel to shopping for a new man.

Men were a little more complicated than snowshoes, but oddly had many of the same qualities. I thought I understood basically how men worked and knew that I'd have to shop around to find the right one. If I got lucky, I might meet someone I could grow to love and decide to make an investment in him that would pay off over time. He'd require some maintenance and care, but in the long run he'd be worth it, because he'd be handy and useful for years to come. The problem with what I learned about snowshoe shopping was that snowshoes are all very similar, but men are not.

Armed with good advice on how to select super snowshoes, I found a great pair of Sherpa Climbers and bought them. I invited my friend Jeanie to snowshoe with me at Mt. Townsend, and we had a great time there. In those days I was a dog sitter for her and her husband Jason. She told me they were going to throw a huge blowout party on New Year's Eve and I was invited. I immediately began to plan my apparel.

On December 31, 1999, I went to a boisterous party at Jeanie's house for the celebration of the millennium. Their home was smack, dab, right on the beach and they had tons of tasty appetizers and a bar that could compete with any nightclub in Seattle. I loaded my plate with shrimp and oysters then asked the bartender to pour me a glass of champagne. The rock music was so astonishingly loud that the only way to talk was to yell into the other person's ear. I had no doubt it would get much louder when Jason wowed us with an incredible display of fireworks.

I was dressed up in a red satin, lace-up corset top with cleavage galore on display and black velvet pants that matched my black velvet open toe heels. I'd bleached my short, spiky hair, but it turned out to be an unnatural yellow and I wondered if I looked too strange. At that time spiky yellow hair was a fashion trend. Even so, no one talked to me and I was surprised.

I camped out near the floor-to-ceiling windows waiting for the fireworks to begin. I sipped on a glass of Cristal champagne my attractive host Jason had just poured and scanned the room. Jeanie was nowhere in sight. I began to think about what the year 2000 meant to me.

I popped a cool juicy oyster with the familiar ocean taste into my mouth and out of nowhere, I remembered something I hadn't thought of for nearly 30 years. When I was twelve, I'd wondered what I'd be like in the year 2000. In 1970 my parents were in their early thirties, and I thought they were old. Compared to them I knew that I'd be an old woman at the age of forty-two. My imagination back then was so far from the current reality of my life. That little twelve-year-old girl was still playing with Barbie dolls and speculated about her decrepit state in the year 2000.

My quiet laugh was lost in the noisy party as I conjured up a mental picture of myself at age 12. I fancied telling my younger self, "You're wrong. You're going to be having the time of your life when you're 42, and if you haven't noticed yet, take a look at this older version of yourself. You're gorgeous and have a body to die for." Just then the fireworks banged and burst into fiery flowers overhead, and my imagined younger self smiled shyly and scampered away.

I'd had too much champagne the night before and suffered one hell of a hangover in the morning. I sat down to check email on my computer, and it worked just fine. A lot of people thought the year 2000 would screw up all the computers. I never believed that would happen, so I wasn't surprised when I had no problems. I checked my inbox and I had got an email from Jake. I was excited because he only emailed to invite me on a hike or climb. That one was an invitation to climb Mt. Ellinor and I was tickled pink. I'd hiked Ellinor in the summer, but never climbed there in the winter. It was a steep hike in the summer, and I'd heard that it was an alpine climb in the winter. I wrote back and asked if I could bring a friend. When Jake replied, okay, I immediately called Cebe and invited him to join us.

I stepped out onto my deck to drink in the salty air, took a few deep breaths and ducked back into my apartment. It was too cold to stand out there for long, but my pounding head seemed a little better. The view from that old wooden deck gave me great pleasure each day, so I stood by the sliding glass door for a while and caught a glimpse of a heron flying down to the water's edge for breakfast.

# ELLINOR AND HER NEIGHBOR

||||||||||||||||||||||||||||||||||||||||||||||||||||||||||||||||||||||||||||||||||||||||||||||||||||||||||

THE DAY BEFORE the climb on Ellinor, I was having lunch at the Streamliner Diner and my good friend Tom Seligh sat down next to me at the counter.

"How's life treating you, Paula?"

"Great and I'm going climbing tomorrow." He cocked his head a little, smiled and continued to look at the menu. "Good for you."

Christina took his order. There were only a few people there because it was a Friday. That place is jammed every weekend, so I only went there on weekdays.

"What's going on with you, Tom?"

"I've just gotten a contract in New York and wonder if you can feed Sparrow while I'm gone?" He had a beautiful cat that always hid from me when I stopped by his apartment.

"Sure." Then he explained he'd be gone for a few months and asked if I could clean the cat box, not my favorite pastime. Tom was a good friend, so I said okay. Then I told him about Mt. Ellinor, but he was distant and when I finished my sandwich. I gave him a hug and said, "Cheer up! It'll be good money and then you'll come back home."

But, he didn't come back home, and moved to Arizona instead of returning to the island. He'd become a close confidant and I really only had one other person I trusted that much. I ended up missing him like crazy.

Mt. Ellinor is right next to Mt. Washington, as you face west toward the Olympic Mountains. On the long drive down we skirted the Hood Canal and where the canal meets the shore, winding channels looked inviting to explore. We met up with Jake at the ranger station, and he followed us up in his car. I felt lucky to be climbing with two of the best climbers I knew. We all stopped at an overlook and I took pictures of Lake Cushman. It resembled a tiny toy model of a campground by a lake. Patches of blue peaked through the cloudy sky, and I hoped for a sunny day.

Around eight in the morning, we parked on the logging road and hiked up. When we got to the 1,000 foot snow chute, there was a lot of recently avalanched snow. Jake and Cebe did an assessment and it looked unstable. That got all of us worried about a possible avalanche, and the solution to that problem was to detour off to one side of the chute.

Using kick steps we climbed an almost vertical wall of snow, and by planting our ice axes firmly in front of us we then pulled ourselves up and repeated that process. It was tough going, but the safest way up. I couldn't stretch my arm out in front of my face without touching that wall of snow. Jake kept dislodging clods of it, and they exploded in my face and one time momentarily blinded me. I wanted to grab his leg and yank him down behind me so he could experience my discomfort. Instead I slowed down and created more distance between us and that helped.

Clouds blocked our view at the top of that ridge, and we'd become disoriented. None of us had gone up that way before, so we stopped and checked the map. I was pretty worn out by then, because climbing the snow wall had been hard work. Jake disappeared ahead of us, and I wondered if we'd be able to make it to the top.

Jake's war whoop rang out, and we joined up with him just minutes later. I could hardly believe we'd made it! Sunshine poured down and we looked across a sea of clouds in layers of pure white, then silver gray depths crowned by the blazing sun. It was a magnificent view as the clouds lifted to reveal Mt. Washington right next to us. Both peaks were dressed in snowy white and a small herd of mountain goats on Washington were nibbling on heaven knows what. The summit of my first climb ever right next to us was literally a cool sight.

Cebe described an interesting traverse from Washington to Elinor that got my imagination going. Jake and I were checking out the ridge connecting those two peaks as Cebe studied his altimeter. He informed us that the barometric pressure was dropping rapidly. The altimeter read 6,400 feet, but we were standing at 5,944 feet, because a low pressure system was approaching. Just then a wall of black clouds blotted out the sun, and we descended so quickly that you'd have thought we'd just robbed a bank. We made a clean getaway and got back to the cars in record time.

Before we left, I asked Cebe if we could go to Logger's Landing, and he was game. I'd asked Jake to join us, but he had plans that evening and couldn't. I was beginning to wonder what that guy was doing in the evening and later learned he loved dancing. The Landing was my favorite place to grab a snack and a beer, and was a home away from home after climbs and hikes in the Olympics.

The long, one-story building always had cars in the parking lot. A football game on the two TVs in the bar drew cheers and hoots from customers there. Clad in ball caps and work clothes, the men in that restaurant reminded me of hanging out with my neighbors at the Four Corners in Mountain Falls, Virginia, my home sweet home.

The Landing might look pretty run down to some people; some of the vinyl chairs had rips or holes in them, but I thought it was comfortable and just plain down-home. It wasn't too crowded; the waitress was pleasant, and they served something I craved. They had the freshest oysters I'd ever eaten, and stopping there was like going home and having good eats, but we didn't have oysters in Mt. Falls.

The Landing is a stone's throw from the Dabob Bay in Quilcene, and from there you could see the water where those oysters came from. The shellfish always tasted as though they'd been plucked from the salty water nearby, because they had been. Oyster shooters weren't on the menu and all the food was fried, but if you asked nicely you could get shooters. The beer was mostly domestic, but they had some good microbrews too. I ordered oysters and an IPA and Cebe asked for a pale ale. I couldn't think of much I'd rather do than just sit there with Cebe, drink, nosh, and soak that place up. I'd always relax there and my batteries would recharge.

Cebe asked,

"How do you like your new Sherpa Climbers?"

"They're the best, and I can run downhill in them. After you gave me advice on good snowshoes, I had no trouble deciding which ones to buy. Are you doing anything with the Mountaineers?"

"I'm working on a couple chapters for the new edition of *Freedom of the Hills*."

"I've heard of it. Should I get a copy?"

"I think it's a good book for anyone who climbs. You know, I haven't been back up Mt. Washington since your training climb there. Maybe you and I should tackle that this winter."

"I'm up for it. I'll join you on a climb anytime." The bartender brought the beer, and a minute later a woman wearing a cook's apron delivered my oysters. I scoffed down my shooters and we toasted each other's company.

Logger's Landing would have been a perfect place for my dad and me to hang out. He would've felt comfortable there. Back home he sometimes took me to the Virginian Restaurant, when I was a teenager, and got pan-fried trout and grits for breakfast. When they closed, Dad was heartbroken, so was I, and I never had fresh trout for breakfast again. Years later, when I flew out to visit him, he'd found a truck stop and it became our new favorite haunt. As an adult, I grew close to him. He passed several years ago, and hanging out in that truck stop eating and swapping stories with him were some of the best times we had.

The oysters were tasty in Quilcene, but I was still hungry when I got home. I didn't want to cook, and decided to walk over to the Winslow Way Cafe. I didn't ever think about calories after I'd done an alpine climb. I ordered a pizza, the big, fat, chocolate cake, and was drinking my second glass of Cab that night, which is normally my limit, when a man sat down next to me.

Terry was a notorious flirt, and was married. One of my clients told me he was putting moves on her. He chatted me up and bought me two more glasses of wine, and for some crazy reason I drank them and regretted it the next day. Terry had a sad sob story that he'd used on my client and was now trying it out on me. I'd heard all kinds of idiotic stories from men who wanted to cheat on their wives. I thought I should just interrupt and tell him to resolve the situation or get a divorce, because "Frankly my dear, I don't give a damn." Instead, I thanked him for the wine and staggered home.

Over the years, I climbed both Ellinor and Washington many times in the winter, because they were so close to my home. I never attempted Mt. Washington in the summer, and gave up on Ellinor as a summer hike when I became a more skilled rock climber. Hiking had been great, but rock or mountain climbing were always my first choices in the warm months. Both of those peaks made good alpine ascents in the winter and kept me tuned up and ready to climb other mountains.

About a month after the climb on Ellinor, Eddy invited me to climb Mt. Washington with him. He was a common friend of Jake's and mine. I loved climbing with Eddy, because he was so laid-back and easygoing, just like my big brother Bill. It was my second climb there. We parked below the trailhead, and had a long hike up the logging road to where the climb started. Having climbed there before, it seemed that it should be less difficult, with emphasis on *seemed*.

The sun beating down on the snow was melting it, but we decided to give it a try anyway, and went up an avalanche gully, where the snow turned to soup. After leading up for about the last 200 feet, I asked Eddy to lead. He didn't want to; in fact, he was certain we should turn around. I pestered him into trying to go a little further, because we were only about 75 feet below the ridge that would take us to the summit, but it wasn't long before Eddy flatly insisted we turn back.

Intently focused on reaching the summit I wanted to swim for it, but with every step we took we'd lose two, and were climbing a giant Slurpee. He said it was just too dangerous for us to keep going up. Of course he was right, but I hated getting so close without finding a way up to the top. I realized later that if we'd continued up, mountain rescue might've had to dig out our bodies. We glissaded down. That's a great way to slide down a snow slope using the ice axe, and it looked like sledding sans the sled. I saw ten to fifteen feet of snow surrounding him begin to move with him. He wasn't aware of that when it first started to happen, until I pointed it out. I'd never seen that happen, and it looked peculiar. He explained that he was making an avalanche! We stopped the glissade and tried to plunge step down, but with each step a bigger area moved with us. It was chilling to think that our descent was beginning to trigger an avalanche, and that we were facing the possibility of being crushed and suffocated under a thunderous wall of white snow.

Eddy said, "Let's try stepping into our footprints." I was in the lead and told him, "I'd like to, but they're covered with avalanche debris." He got down to where I was and we stood there staring blankly at the mess below. We'd obviously missed being buried alive by the skin of our teeth, but neither of us mentioned that obvious fact. Eddy suggested we try to make it down through the woods. It was the only other way out and our last resort.

Well, there was no trail (not even a deer path) in there. We scrambled under branches, over and around rocks, and it was painfully slow. The only reason we didn't feel lost was that we were going steadily downhill and knew we'd eventually come out somewhere on the logging road. Then we came to a full stop and were really stuck. With thick woods behind us, we faced a rocky gully that had a small creek running in it. The only good thing about that situation was that we both stood fully upright for the first time in the past half hour.

Once again we silently assessed our options, and they were few. In a pinch like that, sometimes the best solution is to go ahead and tackle the biggest obstacle. I piped up: "I think we should see if we can cross the creek. That could work for us." Eddy dithered a bit.

"Okay. Let's give it a try." We both continued to do nothing and stared down into a creek bed, about 20 feet below on a steep angle down to snow-covered rocks surrounded by water. I said, "I'll go first," and pictured myself slipping and tumbling in, but thought, "What the heck, I've been hypothermic before and it didn't kill me." He seemed glad I'd volunteered and said in a cheerful voice, "Alright, I'll keep an eye on you." I carefully edged down onto the rocks.

I called up, "So far, so good." And then I slipped, but didn't fall, and reality set in. I knew that if I did fall I'd surely have frostbite by the time I finally got back to my truck. Keeping that in mind, I slowed down and ever so carefully avoided plunging into the freezing water. Once I was all the way down, I excitedly called back, "I made it!" Then I began moving up the other side. Eddy started to head down. Climbing up is always easier than down climbing, so the other side was a breeze, and we were out of the woods literally.

I wished all of my male climbing partners had been more like Eddy. He didn't mind letting me lead, listened to my opinions, and would often try something I suggested. He had an open mind, and treated me with respect. The icing on the cake was that I always felt safe on a climb with him.

Between that climb and the next, I had to focus on my job. I enjoyed helping my clients get in better shape, and my line of work allowed me the leeway I needed to do most of my climbs. During that time in my life, I was always thinking about joining a climbing party. I didn't have any climbs slated for the next few months, so I visited Vertical World more often.

I worked on training plans and asked for referrals because I had to get more clients. Inevitably some would decide they didn't need my services anymore or move away, and one of my favorite places to snag a new client was Bainbridge Bakers.

As I was waiting in line at Bainbridge Bakers to order my latte, a woman walked over and asked me if I ran down Madison Avenue. I told her I did, and she said she'd seen me running and guessed I was a personal trainer. I told her she guessed right, and got hired on the spot. A couple weeks into her workouts, she explained why she wanted to work with me. "I was driving north on Madison and saw you running with such a look of happiness on your face. I wanted to feel like that, and that's why I hired you." She didn't last long, and I suspected that her little bubble of happiness popped when she discovered I'm not all sparkles and light.

While I cooked a salmon filet I'd just bought at Town and Country Market, I was thinking about calling Cebe, to see if he and I could plan a climb. I stopped at T&C every day because it was less than a block from my apartment, so it was basically my refrigerator. As I fixed a big salad, I got a call from Jake. He suggested we get together and talk about a two-week rock climbing trip. What a pick-me-up! I told him that was a great idea, and we made a date to plan it. After I hung up, I realized it was the first time he'd called me. I was sure he could find a guy to do that trip with, and was almost certain he was attracted to me. I thought he might be a slow mover who only needed a nudge.

# LOVE ON THE ROCKS

||||||||||||||||||||||||||||||||||||||||||||||||||||||||||||||||||||||||||||||||||||||||||||||||||||||||||

JAKE SEEMED EAGER to include me in his climbing plans, and I was pretty sure we could be more than climbing partners that year. He had a great sense of humor and was upbeat on all the climbs I'd done with him. He worked as an engineer for the Navy in Bremerton and was twelve years older than me but could be as silly as a kid. What an easy-going guy he was, and I thought what a terrific boyfriend he could be.

The evening I went over to his place, I discovered he had a beautiful home. It was a gray craftsman style house. The yard was manicured, and had red roses that hugged the porch. As I knocked on the door, I could imagine myself caring for him and those rosebushes.

Jake hollered, "The door's open." I saw him doing something in the kitchen. "I'll be out in minute." I walked over to his turntable. I hadn't seen one of those in a long while, and noted that he had an extensive collection of vinyl. I squatted down to read the spines of the albums and saw musicals I was familiar with: *Porgy and Bess*, *Oklahoma*, *The Music Man*, and *South Pacific*. He walked into the room and invited me to sit down. I would've loved to talk about his record collection, but he immediately launched into discussing the trip. We talked about seeing different national parks and doing some climbing in the Southwest. I was revved up and ready to go!

After we figured out how much money we'd each needed to save and looked at maps, I decided it was time to find out if we had the chemistry for a relationship. I was attractive, we loved to do the same sports, and I imagined doing all sorts of things with him. He hadn't tried to initiate a relationship with me, so I worked up the nerve to break the ice.

After discussing the different aspects of the trip, I asked if he was seeing anyone. He said no. Then I snuggled up next to him on the smooth, leather sofa and softly said, "I think we'd make a great couple. Don't you?" Jake recoiled as though he'd been burned by a red hot poker and said, "No!" in a commanding voice. He scolded me like a bad dog, and the temperature of the room seemed to be rising.

"I invited you here to talk about the rock climbing trip. I don't know what's going on with you, but this is the wrong time and place for that question."

I didn't take the hint. We were alone in his large, open living room, and it seemed the perfect time and place to explore our emotional connection. I decided to clear up all the mystery with just one kiss. I scooted back over, leaned in and almost reached my target, when he jumped up from the sofa.

"I don't have those kinds of feelings for you, Paula."

I noted the important word "yet" was missing from that statement. I'd never made a first move on a man before in my life and vowed at that moment never to do it again. My mouth went dry and my tongue was sticking to the roof of it when I said,

" Wh-What should I do now? I feel like a fool."

I was mortified when he replied "Apologize?"

I felt like he should apologize to me for leading me on for so long, but said, "I'm sorry, and I promise there won't be a repeat performance."

"I accept your apology and hope that we can remain friends." Then he walked out of the room!

I was dumbstruck and thought I'd better leave. I dug my truck keys out of my purse and blinked back tears of disappointment. If the only way he looked at me was as a climbing partner, then I'd made a huge mistake and was barking up the wrong tree. I stood there in his beautiful home and took one last look at my vanishing dream then turned and headed to the door. As I was about to turn the handle, he came back into the room.

"Do you have any other questions about our trip?"

I walked toward him, he took a step back and I laid my purse on the sofa. I asked between sniffles, "Do you think we should go on a two-week trip (sniff) together, after what just happened?" He seemed oblivious of the fact that I was sniffling and had red watery eyes.

"We just had a misunderstanding, and that shouldn't affect our trip. I'm ready to forgive and forget, and I hope you are too."

He was so dismissive, but I'd hoped we could defuse the situation a little more. I sat down on the ottoman, and Jake said he had to turn in early and ushered me out the door. I wondered if he thought I was too young for him, or maybe he dreaded dealing with an emotionally charged woman like me. Whatever the reason was he'd basically kicked me out. I didn't understand what was the matter with him. What mattered to me was the feeling that I'd just lost a good friend. I drove to the nearest convenience store to buy a bottle of water and quickly drank it in an effort to soothe some part of myself that was singed.

Even though my advances failed, I wanted to smooth things over in hopes of salvaging our friendship. We had a plan for a great rock climbing adventure beginning at "Frenchman Coulee." That place is a rock climbing mecca in the gorge near George, Washington, and from there we'd head south. I didn't feel the same about Jake after the meeting in his home. I thought he was unpredictable, and I'd become a little afraid of him. I was processing those thoughts when we began our trip.

When all of our equipment was packed into his car, we headed east to the gorge. It was a long drive, and we chatted about our climbing destinations. We made a quick stop in the town of George. It was hot and he didn't have air conditioning in his car. We both got milkshakes. He had strawberry and I had chocolate. I held mine out to him and asked if he wanted some; he shook his head with the straw in his mouth and walked away. I didn't dare ask for a sip of his. They were such refreshing, cold drinks and that was the sweetest part of the next two weeks.

He either had amnesia or was a good actor, because he was pretty much the same old Jake I'd grown to know and love before my embarrassing faux-pas. I had to remind myself more than once that he wanted me to keep my distance. This was the beginning of an adventure with a couple of days of camping and climbing at Frenchman Coulee. After that we'd head south to Smith Rocks in Oregon, San Luis Obispo, California, then on to Las Vegas, Nevada, and finally Boulder, Colorado and with points of interest in between.

As I looked back, I knew he'd wanted to do this trip for years. He'd talked about it the year before. I bet he couldn't find anyone to replace me with on short notice, because if he could have I'm sure he would have. Little did I know at the time that his anger was simmering just below the surface. He actually was a good actor for a couple of days.

I'd never been to Frenchman Coulee before but had heard a lot about it in climbing gyms. I was surprised by the number of people there. I saw about forty people camped in small groups near an unusual rock outcropping called "The Feathers." There was no question why it had that name: huge rocks resembling stone feathers shot up out of the sandy ground.

We got there late in the afternoon, hung out, fixed dinner on our camp stoves, then set up our separate tents. I didn't understand why we didn't share the same tent and stove. I'd done that before on climbs, but never with Jake. I wasn't about to give him any reason to bark at me again and didn't ask.

I ambled around for a while, then climbed into my tent. In the morning, we spent most of the next day climbing the Feathers. There's something for every level of climbing expertise there. Those rock formations had a lot of bolted routes, and were used by sport climbers. The Sunshine Wall only had some anchors for top roping and no bolted routes to clip into. We had a lot of fun at the Feathers and enjoyed watching skillful climbers doing moves that would be very difficult for either of us.

Later that afternoon, Jake and I decided to go find the Sunshine Wall and take a look at potential trad climbs for the following day. We didn't have a map, so it took us a while to get there. We came out at the top of a cliff that dropped almost straight down onto a wide shelf then down into a dry riverbed. Directly opposite, and far away, was the other side of the gorge with huge cliffs that mirrored these. We found a route named Tammy Faye and examined the anchors. They were great and firmly affixed with little rust and no wobbles. We moved on and found other solid anchors along the cliffs. That meant we could spend the next day climbing our butts off! Woo-hoo!

The following day, Jake and I headed to the Sunshine Wall with a friend who was camping nearby named Parker. Jake rappelled from the clifftop to the base of Tammy Faye. His friend Parker and I rappelled down after him, then we climbed to the top without having to place any gear. It was a good start. Parker and I kidded around with each other as we scouted for a while along the base of the cliffs. The rock walls were tightly-packed columns all along the hillside adjoining the riverbed that sloped down far below us.

I had a complete rack of traditional gear ranging from microchips to a size six cam. I'd been purchasing pieces here and there and had built a great rack. I was glad we needed my gear, and it helped us climb a route that had a chimney without anchors at the top. That meant we had to place trad gear as we climbed up. I handed Jake my camera, and he snapped a picture of me climbing there. Later Jake said he was glad I had a size five cam, because we almost never needed one that big in this area, but we might when we got to Colorado. Many climbers only bought gear they'd use frequently.

We didn't see many people on the Sunshine Wall. I guess a lot of them preferred sport climbing and didn't want to invest in trad gear. All my cams were top-of-the-line Black Diamond brand and I knew that owning a trad rack with high quality equipment would increase the size of my playing field and that made it a worthwhile investment. We hardly saw another soul and didn't have to stand around waiting for our turn like we did at the Feathers. No one was in sight and we had our pick of nearly all the rock climbing routes. It just doesn't get much better than that.

Parker heard a couple some distance away using climbing calls. A woman on lead was shouting back to her man who was belaying. We heard her call out "Climbing Babe." And the guys thought it was pretty funny that she called him babe. We climbed 5.6–5.8 comfortably there. The views at the top of the cliffs and across the gorge were awesome, and it was comfortably warm. Together we made a good trio because Parker diffused the tension between Jake and I. I wished he could've come with us, but the next day we had to say goodbye to him and drive south.

# ROCKING AROUND THE SOUTHWEST

||||||||||||||||||||||||||||||||||||||||||||||||||||||||||||||||||||||||||||||||||||||||||||||||||||||||||||||||||||||||||||||||||||||||||||

AS JAKE AND I traveled down into Oregon, I drove through a dense, tall forest of deep green pines that flanked the car on both sides for a long stretch in his Saturn while he snoozed. It was a boring drive that ended late that day at Terrebonne, Oregon, the home of Smith Rock. It's a state park and well known as a fabulous climbing spot to climbers throughout the world. Millions of years ago the biggest volcanic eruption to occur in Oregon created the cliffs we saw. The semi-circular rock ridges jutting up out of a wide-open, flat landscape are all that's left of that volcano.

Hiking around the area we saw a few climbers on the tan cliffs and scrambled a little. It began to rain as we explored cliff walls and had to pack it in. At the time, I didn't realize it was such a special place, and have no idea why we didn't spend a few days there. What Jake wanted Jake got, so we continued down into California the next day. I had no desire to argue with him about anything. We got cheap motel rooms that night, and after all that driving I just sacked out.

The next day we took turns driving, and made it into northern California and ended up somewhere in Mendocino County. By the end of the day we were both burnt out from that long drive. Jake suggested we camp under the stars, and then get going early the next day. That sounded fine to me, but we ran into a problem: no camping areas. He took us down a frontage road and parked in a location that I called, "Where the hell is this!" I could hear the rumble of machinery and the air stank of petroleum. I complained that I didn't like the place and was informed in a stern tone, "We've been driving around looking for a long time, and this is the best we can do." He was angry and frankly I was afraid his behavior might escalate. I had no safe word, so I zipped my lip and grudgingly got into my sleeping bag. I found myself awake most of the night breathing nasty fumes and listening to strange noises in the distance.

In the morning when Jake said it was time to get going, I informed him that I'd hardly slept a wink. He was bright and chipper and found a restaurant where we got some breakfast. I'm sure he must have noticed I was in a funky mood. As we left the restaurant he asked me to drive, and my surly reply was, "Sure, if you want us to get into a wreck." He drove us west on Highway One to the coastline. Right before we got there, I unintentionally added the last bit of fuel needed to set him on fire. I was dozing when he stopped to get gas, and have no idea what I said, but he woke me to ask for our money and suggested I drive. My response must have been far from pleasant. At that point, I'd just ripped off the bandage that covered his true feelings.

I'd been on Coastal Highway One several times, and honestly thought I could drive that stretch of road every day for the rest of my life and never be bored. The coastline is unforgettable! We had a bird's-eye view of the mesmerizing waves of the Pacific Ocean crashing on cliffs below and rolling onto untouched sandy beaches. I noticed while I was absorbed with the landscape that Jake was dead silent, and had the peculiar appearance of someone who'd smelled something very unpleasant. I was finally wide awake and launched into soliloquy about the scenic beauty.

"Look, at the sea and sky! This view is so breathtaking that I think we—"

"Actually, I don't care what you think right now and wish you'd just shut up."

"Huh?! What's wrong?"

"A lot of things. Today you told me you wouldn't drive twice and bit my head off at the gas station."

His words were like a sharp slap. "Oh, wow! I'm sorry. I, w-was really bushed because I hadn't slept."

"Guess what? I was too, but I didn't chew you out, and I've done *all* the driving today—"

I interrupted, "Just pull over and I'll drive."

"There's no pull out anytime soon, so I'll have to keep driving."

"Okay. I'm sorry."

"Can it." We didn't talk again until we got close to Morro Bay.

We'd been traveling in stifling silence for hours and were nearing my old stomping grounds, where we'd begin our southwestern climbing spree, and the sign for San Simeon appeared. I became animated and declared that Hearst Castle is a must see. "Jake, it looks like it came straight out of a fairytale. The owner imported exotic animals and I know some still live there." As we got closer, I bounced on the seat while I repeatedly pointed at the hillside and shouted "Look, look — you can see zebras!" He pushed my hand out of the way. I hadn't noticed in my frenzy that it was right in front of his face. His expression was one of utter boredom as he looked over at the zebras but didn't slow down. Jake couldn't have been more blasé' as he yawned and said blandly that we didn't have time for it. So, he shut me down again, and as we drove past the monolith of Morro Rock, nary a peep escaped my lips.

I'd contacted my dear friend Annette before Jake and I took off and asked if we could spend a night in her home. She was happy to have us, and we were warmly welcomed there. She still lived in the same attractive house, on the outskirts of San Luis Obispo, where she'd been living when I moved away. We'd become good friends at library story time, when I was 7 months pregnant with my middle son Willy, and had my 3 year old son Matt on my lap. She'd been sitting next to us with her adorable daughter, Michelle. That had been fifteen years before.

Annette and I took a long walk up into the conical, golden hills behind her home. The grass that covered them appeared groomed, and I could see cattle below that served as the lawnmowers. Dirt paths spiraled up and around the hillsides that were dotted with California Oaks. We walked and talked in the soothing landscape that exuded an air of peacefulness.

I gave her the whole story about Jake. She listened attentively nodding now and then, "Paula, you're barking up the wrong tree. Jake isn't attracted to you, and I don't think he's your friend anymore."

"We were good friends, and I want to make it right."

"That's not going to happen, if you keep trying to fix it you could make things worse. You should brace yourself for more unpleasantness from him and don't expect much else."

"I'd forgive a man who made a move on me that I rejected with no problem. I only hope to be his friend and climbing partner now."

"That's you. He'd be treating you differently by now if he intended to mend fences with you."

"I was afraid of that, Annette."

San Louie is near and dear to my heart, and after that walk with my dear friend, I was reminded of what I was missing and felt a prick of anguish.

After dinner that evening, I walked barefoot onto the flagstone patio behind her house and kicked back in an Adirondack chair. The air was soft and warm, and my eyes were drawn again to the hills. I saw a line of cattle slowly making their way single file up the narrow, coiled path. A small water fountain was near the chair, and I relaxed and let my mind drift.

With closed eyes, I listened to the soothing sound of the water and remembered lying in a field that sloped down to the creek on our farm. The sky opened in a wide infinite field of blue, and I was drenched with warm sun. My view was painted with long blades of grass and the fresh scent of timothy hay floated in the light wind. I was connected to that place. The warm breeze ruffled my hair as I sat up and watched mayflies dancing just above the surface of the creek, until a big blue dragonfly zoomed in and scattered them all. I heard the sounds of frogs croaking, crows cawing, and far away over the fields Annette called to me, "Paula, Paula, wake up! Come in. I have dessert." Snap, I woke up. Later that night I got the best sleep I'd had in a while on a real bed.

I'd begun subscribing to a climbing magazine right after I'd read that great article about Lynn Hill, and they regularly had the beta (route descriptions) on rock routes around the U.S. I'd found what I thought would be an interesting route to do in San Luis, tore out the pages, and brought them with me.

Jake and I looked it over at Frenchman Coulee and had planned to do it, but I was more than a little worried that he wouldn't climb with me anymore. The next morning, although he'd barely spoken to me, he was coiling the rope and getting ready to go. We left Annette's house and went to an area near Questa College.

We didn't think anyone had ever climbed there, and wondered if we were in the right place, because the rock features were intermittently covered with foliage. We managed to climb a couple of pitches, but on the way up there was a lot of gardening going on. We didn't think much of it, but at least it was a climb. We saw poison ivy as we left and didn't touch it, but the rope did. Back at Annette's Jake washed the rope in her bathtub. We spent a relaxing evening with her, and I got another good night's sleep. The next morning Annette and I said goodbye, and we both thanked her and headed east to Nevada.

As we drove across the desert in California on the way to Las Vegas, I asked Jake If we were on the same highway where James Dean had crashed his car and died. Dean was often cast as a rebel in old movies, and I liked the way he played that part. Jake replied with a grunt. I'd been listening to that same monosyllabic reply all morning.

I drove most of the time we were in the California desert and the whole time we were in Nevada. That was fair, since he'd driven us all the way down the California coast. Jake woke up as I sped on the highway and took a sharp curve that made his head smack right into the window. He gave me a grim look and said, "I'm sleeping over here. Do you think you could take it easy?" I slowed down, and considered that this was the closest thing to a conversation we'd had all day. Coming into Las Vegas we were in-stop-and-go traffic. I had no interest in that city, mostly because our destination was Red Rocks and partly because the memory I had of that place had left a nasty taste in my mouth.

When we were kids my parents took my brother and me to visit friends who lived in Las Vegas. My mom's girlfriend was a showgirl who worked in a large casino. Both of my parents were heavy drinkers at that time and so was the showgirl and her husband. Seeing them when they came home from the casino one evening was confusing and scary when I was seven.

I got us to the campground at Red Rocks just outside of Las Vegas, where we set up tents and got out our cookware. We planned to sleep there and try to do some climbs the next day. Why we didn't have any route maps I don't know. Maybe Jake had thought we'd get the skinny from other climbers, but I wasn't about to ask. I noticed there were few people in the area. The campground was an arid flat that was full of tumbleweeds and dotted with yuccas. I only have one good photo of Red Rocks that Jake took of me in our campground. In fact it may be the only picture I have from that trip. Of course, I do have great postcard pictures of it, and all of the other places we visited on that journey. Tall hills flanked the climbing area, and near us were a bevy of low copper-colored rock formations we'd investigate.

Next morning, the weather was fine. We got dressed, ate, grabbed our climbing gear and went to the information center. They didn't know diddly about climbing routes, so we took off and started scanning the sandstone cliffs for other climbers. We walked up into an area with huge, rounded rock formations the color of raw sienna. I remember hopping around barefoot on the warm surface of an enormous boulder that resembled a giant inverted, reddish-brown soup bowl. I loved the feel of the rock, because it was similar to fine grit sandpaper and when I climbed the sandstone cliffs there, the surface somehow fooled my brain into thinking it felt soft.

Jake and I managed to do a couple of single pitch climbs, then began to look for a new route. He noticed some guys who seemed to be in trouble. One of their party was stranded high above them. Two men on the ground yelled up to a man high above on a rock shelf. Those men were visiting from Canada. The man who was stranded had free soloed up that rock wall and couldn't come down. Free solo means he went up there with no rope or protection of any kind. That's something I don't recommend doing. He apparently didn't know that it's always much harder to come down than to climb up, and he'd bitten off more than he could chew.

Jake figured out how to rescue him. The top of the rock where the man was stranded looked about 30 feet up, and he was able to help him climb down with the aid of a rope. I can't say how Jake got the rope up to him, because I was too busy chatting it up with one of the Canadians.

I watched as they celebrated their friend's return to flat ground. Those guys were pretty thrilled with Jake's help, thanking him over and over while clapping him on the back. I exchanged email addresses with my new Canadian friend Jean, because I thought it might be fun to climb in Canada someday.

The rescue effort burned up the last of our daylight. Then Jake confessed he'd always wanted to eat a steak at a restaurant in Las Vegas. I loved steak too, so we got cleaned up and headed into town. That seemed to lift his spirits, Thank God! He'd been such a bear for the last few days. We actually had some pleasant conversation during that meal. As we left that restaurant, I saw a couple who were stumbling drunks, that refreshed the disturbing image of my alcoholic parents. I hoped to return to Red Rocks someday, but I'd make a point of avoiding Las Vegas altogether.

We went back to camp, and the next morning packed up to leave! We'd done almost nothing! With just two routes under our belts at Red Rocks, a miserable climb in San Luis Obispo, and a cruddy little scramble at Smith Rocks, I was aghast. Both Smith Rock and Red Rocks were huge climbing meccas and we'd hardly touched them! I knew we'd eventually get to Boulder, but had no idea what we'd do there. I thought that I was really wasting my time on that trip, but had to remind myself that Jake had stressed his interest in visiting national parks. I suspected Jake of doing as little climbing as possible with me.

From Las Vegas we went to The Valley of Fire. If Red Rocks was pretty with orange red sandstone, then The Valley of Fire was phenomenal. Rock formations with layers of off-white and red stone were all around us. They reminded me of a red velvet cake with layers of white cream filling. We went into the information center, learned about the Anasazi Indian migrations and took a hike to see the petroglyphs that the Anasazi left for other tribe members during a mass migration. Most of the artful messages were still crisp and clear! I was glad Jake had taken me there, and it was a wonderful sidebar to our climbing trip.

That was a day of amazing sights, and it lifted my sinking spirits. We got back onto our old friend Highway 15 and entered Utah. At Zion National Park we got an eyeful of cliffs that shot up 500-2,000 feet around us. Jake explained it was big wall climbing and we didn't have the equipment or skill to do that. We continued on and entered Bryce Canyon National Park just in the nick of time and set up our tents in failing light.

The next morning, Jake and I did some hiking in Bryce. Wow, what amazing rock formations! Dr. Seuss must have been the architect of the Hoodoos. They were tall, irregularly shaped rock obelisks, and reminded me of something a kid playing in the mud might make. One spot that impressed me had a dazzling white wall of sandstone that projected at a 90 degree angle from the hillside. At my eye level there was an oval shaped hole. I guess it was formed by wind and rain. The perfectly clear blue sky was framed by that rock window. As I looked at it in wonder, a small Colorado blue bird perched in it, spied me, and flew away. It might not sound like much, but you had to be there. We didn't climb there — just hiked.

The next day we drove through Capitol Reef; we didn't see another soul that day and that place was incredible! It was an enormous desert punctuated with mesas the size of huge buildings, and lived up to its name with rock formations resembling the White House. It was a long drive through there and made me feel that we were the last two people on earth.

Jake warned me that it would be rough going and he wasn't kidding. I just hoped the car would clear all the big rocks on the dirt road, and was afraid that we'd get stuck. We banged along on that rocky road in Jake's Toyota, and one time he scraped the length of the undercarriage, but he did get us through there. From Capitol Reef National Park we headed toward Moab.

Utah's scenery was captivating, the houses that dotted the road were the quintessential relics of a farm era gone by. The homes I saw were well maintained; old clapboard buildings and the fields that surrounded them made me homesick.

As beautiful as it was, the coffee was the worst I'd ever tasted. Living in the Seattle area I'd grown to appreciate good java. I'm no aficionado, but will go to great lengths to procure an outstanding cup of Joe at the mere mention of it. Every time we stopped for gas or to use the bathroom I tried to get a cup of coffee. If I could find it, it was usually burnt sludge at the bottom of a pot, or decaf. I can't drink sludge or the weakest excuse for coffee, so I just had to give it up for a while.

Hiking up to the Arches in Moab was a treat. No one could climb on the most famous rocks there because they could be damaged by climbers and their gear. My favorite formation was named "Delicate Arch." In some places the rock thinned so much that it seemed the top could tumble down at any moment. On the way up there I had a view of the Monte La Salle mountains in the distance, and they held some mystery for me. I can't put my finger on why, but as I looked past the rock arches a vast desert plain spread to the base of those snow-capped mountains and I found them simply fascinating.

While we were tooling around in the town of Moab, Jake confessed that when we were at Annette's, he'd been thinking about buying a plane ticket and sending me home. That didn't come as a surprise to me because I thought he was on the verge of strangling me most of the time. I'd kept apologizing until we hit Las Vegas, and then he'd firmly insisted that I quit.

I didn't respond to his admission that he'd rather I wasn't there, because what could I say. I nodded and stoically carried on. I knew things weren't the same, but I also knew he wouldn't have done any rock climbing without me. Still when I considered how little climbing we'd done, it didn't pan out as a climbing vacation, because we were mostly just sightseeing.

We'd just tolerated each other ever since we got on Highway One in California. I actually think that he'd barely managed to put up with me ever since I'd tried to steal a kiss from him. The reality of Jake and I was that our friendship was truly over.

We left Moab and drove north to Boulder, Colorado. We stopped and parked near the cute pedestrian-only downtown. The street was closed to cars and the open shopping area was festive and upbeat. The shops were mostly local boutiques. We went to an ice cream parlor and enjoyed giant cones, then walked all around and were refreshed by the sights and sounds of that lively, upscale place. I noticed that in addition to steak, ice cream also seemed to lift his spirits briefly. I wished I could pass that information about his food preferences on to his future wife so she could soothe his hot head.

When we went to the Flat Irons, a climbing area in Boulder, I thought he might let me place some trad pro there, but I discovered that he'd rather run his mother over with a truck. My big cams were a good thing to have there, and Jake did have the beta on that place. We climbed a route called Fandango, which took most of the day, and that steep rock wall resembled one side of a pyramid.

Close to the top when I looked back, there was Boulder below me, and the trees spread into the distance until they disappeared where the earth met the sky. That place had a timeless quality and a view of infinity. After we reached the top we simply hiked and scrambled down the other side.

We walked back to the car, and I was wiped out and couldn't wait to hit the hay. We'd rented a motel room with two queen beds, took showers, and watched TV. The walls of that room were permeated with Jake's dislike of me. It was oppressive having to share the room with him, and I couldn't wait to get home the next day.

On the drive through Wyoming the following day, the wide open prairies made me think of cowboys on horseback. Just outside of Bozeman, Montana, I saw a bay and some chestnut horses out at pasture. The bay in that field could've been my Zack's twin.

We had about twenty acres in timothy hay on our family farm in Virginia, and I loved the smell of it. In the hayloft on sunny afternoons, the light filtered in and turned it into a kind of golden heaven, especially when I kicked the hay and tiny bits turned into stardust. Up there, if my horse kicked up a fuss I'd usually let him out in the field. Sometimes he managed to run away, and I never figured out how he got out of that fenced pasture. I'd go looking for him and ride him home bareback. When he ran off like that, I had a good idea of where he was, because even though he was gelded I usually found him ogling the mares down at the Crocker's farm. He had good taste in women; the Crocker family had some beautiful thoroughbreds.

Driving home was a straight shot from Bozeman on Interstate 90. Another good thing about that day, besides seeing Zack's twin, was going over the continental divide. At over 6,000 feet, it's forested with gnarly little pine trees and gave us a sweeping view as we dropped down its western slope.

On the way home I thought I'd weathered that trip pretty well, all things considered. Jake had been so unforgiving. I wondered what had turned him into the caustic man I'd gotten to know, because I had my demons too.

My life turned upside down when my family disintegrated and lost the farm. I'd ended up joining the Army to escape the whole mess. The upside of that was, I don't put much stock in personal possessions, and travel light. On the downside, it's hard for me to form friendships and harder still to forgive a personal injury...just like hardheaded Jake.

We pulled up to my apartment, and Jake divided our remaining funds, then said, "Here's your half of what's left." I took it and didn't even bother to look at it. I got out of the car, and he'd already popped the trunk. When I closed it, he drove off, and hadn't bothered to say goodbye. I assumed I'd never see or hear from him again, because during our travels I'd suspected there would be no fond farewells. The after-effect of our escapades was similar to having just gotten off a rollercoaster ride that made me want to puke, and I was glad it was over.

Shortly after rock climbing in the Southwest, I was invited by Cebe to climb Mt. Rainier again! He told me we were going to get Jenny to the top this time. I had my doubts about that, but was more than ready to try.

*Previous page:* Paula, a few days before her first attempt on Mt. Rainier (photo: D.J. Johnson).

*Above:* Climbing Mt. Ellinor (photo: Cebe Wallace).

*Next page:* A challenging rock climb at Little Si.

Frenchman Coulee May 2000

*Above:* Taking in the view on the Sunshine Wall in Frenchman Coulee.

*Right:* Paula standing on the summit of The Brothers.

*Next page:* Belaying in Mission Creek Canyon, Cashmere, WA.

*Previous page:* Paula's first climb on the Flat Irons in Boulder, CO.

*Above:* Hiking up Mt. Shasta.

*Next page:* Paula's Victory Salute on her first summit on Mt. Rainier (photo: Cebe Wallace).

# THE RENAISSANCE MAN AND
# THE SECOND TIME AROUND

||||||||||||||||||||||||||||||||||||||||||||||||||||||||||||||||||||||||||||||||||||||||||||||||||||||||||||||||||||||||||||||

I DECIDED TO do endurance training to prepare for the upcoming climb. As I came around the corner to the free weights area, I saw a powerful body in motion. Most people want someone to spot them or use a personal trainer when they do heavy lifts, but that man was working out alone. He'd definitely caught my eye, but not because he was lifting heavy. In a word, that man was hot!

I had to get away from him, because I knew that I'd keep staring at him and didn't want to get caught doing that. So I used the cable machine and that was about as far away as I could get from him. Then I remembered my second husband David had once mentioned that he'd met a man named Ryan in the gym. David had given me a quick sketch of Ryan's appearance, and the sexy guy I'd just seen matched David's description. I wondered if he was the same man and that gave me a good excuse to go back over and check him out.

I watched as he racked the weights, and his eyes met mine. He smiled and said hi. I was tongue tied, quickly looked away and barely managed to squeak out, hi in return.

"It's nice to meet you, Paula." I felt even more disturbed, realizing he knew who I was. "My name's Ryan."

I wore spandex capris, a jog bra, sneakers and that's it. His eyes roved over me as he spoke. His muscular physique would be best described as a work of art.

We had a brief conversation, and he mentioned that he lived on a sailboat, then he had to go to work. After he left and I calmed down, the thought occurred to me that a lot of people knew my name in the gym, because there were only a few personal trainers who worked there. I'd taken note of the fact that Ryan wasn't wearing a wedding band, and decided to keep an eye out for him in the gym, but as the weeks rolled by I didn't see a trace of him.

I wasn't about to stalk him at the dock because that would be too weird. Instead, I started hanging out at the Pegasus Coffee shop in the mornings between my appointments, because a lot of men with boats in the marina had breakfast there. Plan B was to make frequent kayak trips in the harbor in hopes of seeing him onboard his boat. He'd made an impression on me, and I was determined to see him again.

Having coffee at Pegasus paid off after my third attempt. I found Michelangelo's living sculpture as he sipped coffee alone at a table for two. I pretended not to see him, got a latte, and started looking around for a place to sit. He said, "Hi Paula, care to join me?'

"Oh Ryan, what a nice surprise," I lied. I mentioned that I hadn't seen him in the gym lately. He said he was working two jobs and really didn't have time to lift.

As we talked, I studied his face, and ohhh, what a face he had. His well-tanned, attractive facial features were framed by dark hair with a touch of gray at the temples, and I thought, "I could just eat him right up," I wondered if this might go somewhere, but I had an appointment at the gym and took my coffee cup to the dishpan. He asked me what I was doing later, and I told him not much. That day I only had a couple of appointments before 1 p.m. Then he asked me if I'd like to check out his boat. I was doing my best not to let on that I was absolutely crazy about him and didn't answer right away. Then I said as nonchalantly as I could, "That sounds cool." We made a date to meet later at the public dock.

I had the worst time ever at work and was distracted, because I couldn't wait to get out of the gym. I was thinking about what I'd wear on Ryan's boat, when my client Amelia said, "Hey wake up...I finished my leg presses five minutes ago, and you didn't say a thing, so I just did two more sets." I apologized profusely because she was one of my best clients and deserved all my attention. I focused on her and talked to her about her workout until our session was over. That was my last appointment that day. Thank god!

When I got home from the gym, I took a shower, put on a tight pair of jeans and a form-fitting tank top. It was a warm, cloudless day, and as I walked past the sandy beach next to the public dock, I saw a woman and a little boy building a sandcastle together. Fish darted under the gray, weathered wooden dock and seaweed floated nearby. That part of the harbor was filled with boats from the yacht club, and many were floating out at anchor. There was a light breeze, and when I spotted Ryan, my heart leapt. I was definitely in lust. He tied up his wooden dinghy. I told him "I like your boat." In the marina, that's code for I like you, but it didn't seem to register, because his response was, "I built it."

Once we were on his sailboat, Ryan started to show me around and I saw that it was special. I'd only been on sailboats that were mostly fiberglass, and this one well, it was all wood. Ryan led me up to the bow, and I thought I heard him say he'd built this boat. I came to a full stop and said incredulously, "You built *this*?" He told me he'd dreamed about it since he was a little boy and building it had always been a goal. I was impressed, and then he wowed me when he told me it had been on the cover of *Fine Woodworking*. I began to notice he spoke in an almost toneless monosyllabic manner, but he set me at ease with a knock-your-socks-off smile right about then.

The interior of his boat was surprisingly neat for a bachelor pad, and the warm wood curved to fit the borders of the hull. It was an attractive wooden home for one. We went back up on the deck and he asked me if I had the rest of the afternoon free. When I told him I did, we went out for a short sail.

About the time the wind completely died, he informed me the sailboat didn't have a motor or an outboard motor either. I was amazed because everyone had a motor. I got a little worried and said, "Now what, do we lean over and paddle?"

He gave me another million dollar grin, produced cold beer and said, "Now we float."

Floating was a good thing and I wanted to float away to Shangri-la with him and never return. We drank a couple beers and sadly the wind picked up. Then he took me back to the dock and waved goodbye.

As much as I wanted to spend an eternity exploring this man's gorgeous body, he was too polite and socially distant for that to ever happen. He never made a move on me and didn't even flirt. I was so disappointed. Why had he invited me to his boat? What were his intentions? Would I ever hear from him again? I didn't know the answer to any of those questions, but I did know one thing for sure. I wished we were still floating, because at this point we were dead in the water. I was a shoe girl and it occurred to me that we weren't well suited as a couple, his boat was too small for all of my shoes, so I dismissed all thoughts of him.

I was prepared to climb Rainier again and had no doubt that my second climb there would be better than the first. I wasn't worried about trying to do anything out of the ordinary and was sure that we'd summit. I knew I'd be more considerate of the members in our climbing party, even though I hadn't met a couple of them.

Cebe told me Jenny was determined to get to the top this time, despite her apparent altitude sickness the first time she attempted Mt. Rainier. We'd take a different route this time, and that could make it more challenging, but I really had a good feeling about the whole thing. I was confident in my ability and told myself I'd be far more comfortable with all my clothes on.

Cebe drove and we made a much needed stop at Krispy Kreme Donuts. Normally Cebe and I were conscious of healthy eating, but we also had a real weakness for donuts. We agreed that we could eat anything we wanted the day before going up Rainier and we did! I pigged out on lemon-filled powdered sugar donuts and cruised on the sugar high all the way to the campground.

The sky was clear, and I thought "Great! Maybe we could start today." As we got closer to the White River campground, we knew we wouldn't be starting up anytime soon. There was a huge lenticular cap on the top of the mountain. That's a cloud formation that basically has its own weather system. It could be clear and beautiful all around Rainier, but the wind could be blowing at one hundred miles per hour in whiteout conditions inside that cloud cap.

We got to the campsite at 4,400 feet and rendez-voused with the rest of our group. This time, Jenny came with her husband and a car full of camping gear. Her hubby was planning on hanging around until she descended so we could all celebrate together. Cebe explained that we'd wait a couple of days and see if the cap blew off. Everyone in our group decided to stay and wait it out.

After we'd all set up camp, Cebe invited us to join him in a mock glacier rescue. He wanted us to learn how to rescue someone who'd fallen into a crevasse and was dangling on the rope. He took us through the procedure step by step. It was good to observe, but I knew I needed to practice that myself. When I got home I did practice it with a sack of potatoes on the balcony of my apartment. We all had our individual meals and called it a night.

The next morning, the cap was still there, but it was beginning to blow off the top of Mt. Rainier a little. Cebe made a judgment call and said it would take us a whole day to make the high camp and the better part of the next day to summit. The cap was moving off, so he thought we could begin our journey. Everyone was overjoyed with that news. The young couple that I'd just met the day before were jumping up and down and we all hooted and hollered. We were about to begin our trek up.

We quickly downed coffee and breakfast, packed up and headed out. Cebe had warned us that this was a long approach, and boy he wasn't kidding. We hiked a long way in the woods and then skirted the mountain on a pile of rock rubble known as a moraine. While we were on the moraine before we'd gone up anything very steep, Jenny couldn't keep up, and I thought that was weird, because we'd hardly gained any elevation. Cebe egged her on, but she looked completely whipped. That was when we all took some of her gear, and that seemed to help her a lot.

After hours of hiking we got to the Inter Glacier. It shot straight up in front of us, and at the base of it there was a little stream. We all put on climbing harnesses, tied into the ropes, donned our helmets and got crampons on. With ice axes in hand the most difficult part of this climb began.

You might wonder why climbers wear helmets on a glacier. A smooth field of snow on a glacier can be hiding a cavernous crevasse. If one of the members on a rope steps onto a snow-covered crevasse, and then yells "falling," as they disappear into it, the rest of the rope team ideally dives into the ice axe arrest position. The one who fell into the crevasse will suddenly be jerked to a stop. Sometimes when that happens, the fallen climber smacks against the ice walls of the crevasse. Without a helmet, they could be knocked unconscious. Picture trying to rescue someone who is dead weight and unresponsive. The brain bucket will also keep your head together if you fall on rocks.

Moving up the glacier, someone cracked open a roll of Lifesavers and positioned them on the snow ledge that was about hip height. They were spaced about a foot apart. I just love fruit flavored Lifesavers and started eating them all up, but was severely chastised, because unbeknownst to me those were incentive candies for Jenny. When I heard that I remembered I'd used that tactic on my toddlers.

It wasn't too long, after I started carrying the extra load from Jenny's gear in my pack, that my left shoulder started to ache. I'd injured it years before when I lifted a heavy case of wine at work, and I hardly ever noticed it, but at that time it was painful. When we took a lunch break at Camp Curtis, I was in agony and my shoulder was throbbing. I told Cebe my shoulder hurt, and he distributed the extra gear I carried to the others.

From Camp Curtis, we headed up toward our high camp at Camp Schurman on Steamboat Prow. A lot of the snow had melted away from the rocky mountainside. We went back downhill to reach the high camp and that seemed strange, but that's what you need to do on that route. We dipped down into some steep volcanic rubble, then went back up toward Steamboat Prow. The journey took more time than I'd expected, because it was a long approach under the weight of a heavy pack. As the crow flies, that high camp is only about six miles from the White River campground.

I was at the end of our rope team, and as we neared high camp I could see that we had to take a big leap over what must be a crevasse. I've mentioned that I don't like to jump when climbing. That jump was nightmarish for me. When I got close enough to see down into it, I was scared stiff. It was about three feet wide, and normally that wouldn't be a problem, but I was carrying close to half my body weight in my pack.

Talk about jumpy! I was so nervous about leaping over that damn crack in the ice that I just wanted to turn and run. The others looked like they were doing it without a care. Keep in mind that I was the shortest person in our group, but I didn't have a choice, since it was the only way to get to Camp Schurman. So ever the tough girl, I didn't voice my concerns at all and figured the worst thing that might happen would be that I'd learn all about crevasse rescue from the wrong end of the rope.

When I had to jump, I hesitated, took a couple steps back to get a running start and leaped over as far as I could. I couldn't believe it when I barely managed to clear it. Later I confessed to Cebe that jumping that crevasse was a hellish experience for me.

We set up camp and did the usual early chow and early to bed routine. On the way up that day, the dangerous cloud cap continued moving off the summit. In the morning we'd know for sure if we could attempt it, and went to bed with high hopes.

Up until this climb, my three season tent had been fine, but I was about to learn why I needed a four-season tent. I'd never minded that it wasn't warm, but on *that* night sleeping inside a plastic grocery bag in a windstorm would've been just as comfortable. All night long, a strong steady wind whipped the tent walls. They crackled and crinkled, as they shook hard in the wind. If the noise wasn't enough to keep us awake, the nearly collapsing sides of the tent were. They were constantly smacking Jenny and me in the face. We twisted and turned, fidgeted and scrunched until we eventually worked in tandem to create a brace with our bodies that at least kept the tent walls off our faces. My shoulder throbbed all night long, and I don't think either of us got any sleep that night.

There was only one good thing about that windy night. The wind blew the cloud cap off the summit, and began to drop by morning. I probably could have caught a couple of z's, but was way too excited about reaching the summit to sleep at daybreak. After coffee, I stopped and eagerly asked Cebe, "When are we going?" The winds were only gusting at times, and we saw clouds hugging the mountain between us and the summit, but the top was clear. He decided we should wait at least another hour. I was less than thrilled with that decision, but decided to keep my mouth shut. I was having some bad thoughts, but hadn't said anything unpleasant yet.

During that hour, we prepared to go and then tied into our rope teams. I was part of a rope team of three, with a guy who had a camera in the lead followed by his wife in the middle. She'd been pleasant to talk to on the way up, and when she got overheated on the moraine, I let her borrow one of two light weight sport tops in my pack. The sun reflected on the glacier, and even though we were surrounded by snow and ice all of us got hot there.

The cloud cover began to melt away on our ascent, with the help of occasional gusts of wind. When we'd started out, there was almost no visibility. Another climbing team came up behind us, and I got to chat with their leader, Scott. He was really cute and hailed from Colorado. We were flirting steadily on the way up, and he said he'd like to climb with me sometime. As soon as he uttered those words, my man finder kicked into high gear. At lightning speed, I got my Altoid can, pulled the paper liner out, grabbed my lip liner, and jotted down my contact information for him. He gave me a warm smile and disappeared back into the clouds. After he and his team passed us, I didn't see him again on that trip. Lip liner and Altoids are nonessential gear. I rarely wear makeup, but lipstick was a must for me if I was going to be in a summit photo. Altoids aren't necessary, but I have them with me at all times. I had fresh, minty breath and a beautiful smile when I met Scott. So ladies, remember, be prepared because you never know when or where you might meet the one.

The clouds had completely vanished and I saw the magnificent sunrise on Rainier for the second time. It was a beautiful gift from heaven. The guy with the camera had never been up there before, so he spent a lot of time — and I mean an awful lot of time — taking pictures. That meant everyone had to repeatedly stop and stand still every time he had the whim to shoot. It made no sense to me at all that he was allowed to do that. Our climbing pace was in the hands of a novice who appeared to be more intent on taking photos than reaching the summit, and I wondered why our climb leader didn't quash that behavior. I later learned that Cebe was close friends with the camera guy's dad.

Every time he decided to take a picture, I got angrier, and I even had to stop and watch him refill the film! I know I said something to him about slowing us down, and his response, which I will never forget was, "I'm a photographer, and I need to record this."

I told him, "I don't know if you've noticed it or not, but we're on a climb, not a photo shoot!" I understood the desire to record his summit bid on Mt. Rainier, but wanted more than anything to focus on climbing. He completely ignored me, and his frequent stops turned up the heat on my simmering anger.

We were moving up a glacier at that time. I'd figured out when I climbed Shuksan that I stay nice and warm if I have a comfortable pace and keep moving on ice. When forced to stop frequently on a glacier for more than a short time, I chilled down fast. That guy with the camera was, in my opinion, a selfish bastard who was effectively spoiling the quality of my summit experience.

When we finally had the summit in sight, I asked Cebe if I could go ahead of the group. He didn't like that idea too much, but as soon as we were on the crater rim he said go ahead. I ran to Columbia Crest because I had so much pent-up negative energy. Just like this volcanic peak, I needed to blow off some steam. I highly recommend *never running* on the summit of Mt. Rainier. I would never do it again. The headache I got was a whopper and didn't subside until we headed back down.

I remembered seeing those two men running toward the summit when I got my nude picture there the year before. The thought occurred to me that the reason they didn't get to the summit while I was there was that they'd been slammed with splitting headaches.

Most of the party took summit pictures, but not me. I didn't do that unless it's unique or special to me in some way. I only have a couple of summit photos in my journal. When everyone had taken pictures and reveled in the moment, we headed back down to Steamboat Prow. I was still at the end of the rope team. The descent was humdrum, and when we got to our camp Cebe took a vote to see who wanted to stay the night and who wanted to descend. I think both Jenny and I voted to descend, but guess who we were out-voted by. The married couple wanted to stay and Cebe who had the swing vote put his hand up after they raised theirs, so we all had to stay another night.

In the morning, Jenny and I were getting dressed to go on down, and to say that I smelled was an outright lie. My powerful stench reeked in every corner of the tent, and I'm sure it could've knocked a strong man down. That was day four without a shower, and we had sweat heavily on all of those days. I'd liberally used antiperspirant every morning and my armpits weren't half bad, but the rest of my body emitted a toxic stench. I told Jenny I was glad I had her as my tent mate because, "No man could put up with me today. Oh God, I just stink!" Fortunately, no one came near me that day.

On the way down from our high camp, I was in the lead position for a change on my rope team, followed by the camera guy and his wife, sport-top girl. The camera guy didn't mind my pace because he'd used all his film on the way up. His wife, on the other hand, at the end of our rope kept asking me to slow down. Like me on the way up, she was at the end of her rope on the way down. All the minor irritations had festered long enough, and I was a bitch on ice. Her incessant whining pushed me over the edge, and I lost it. I stopped, turned around, and said, "What's your problem?"

"You need to slow down. I feel like you're dragging me down the mountain, and I might fall."

"I'm not going fast, and if you do fall you'll just land on your big fat ass."

You wouldn't believe the expression of hatred on her face. I was angry and wanted to piss her off. Those words weren't premeditated and just tumbled right out. I didn't care how she felt and was sick of her complaining! In my defense — and it's a weak one — I could've said worse things.

We had to jump some narrow crevasses that we'd encountered on the way up, plus a few new ones. As we got closer to the base of the glacier, eventually the crevasses vanished, and I saw an opportunity for a little fun. I asked Cebe if I could glissade. He told me mountaineers never glissade on glaciers.

I've described why we wore helmets. Now envision that a climber is not on a rope team, they're sliding down a slope at top speed, and suddenly disappear vertically into a crevasse. The best thing you can do is just sing the hallelujah chorus and kiss them goodbye. I'm sure this unpleasant thought crossed Cebe's mind, but he must've seen what I saw. We were so close to the base of the glacier. Then he acknowledged that this wasn't a Seattle Mountaineers-sponsored climb and let me go for it. I didn't know much about the Seattle Mountaineers Club then. I knew Cebe was a respected member, but I hadn't really looked into it, yet.

While I was untying the rope, I noticed cameraman and his wife had begun to coil it up. I assumed they'd safely plunge step down after me. I had to keep my helmet on to please Cebe. I let out my typical "Yahoo!" as I sailed down a long stretch of snow that was maybe two hundred feet to the base of the glacier. I used my ice axe to guide me on that glissade, but didn't brake until I almost hit the rocks, and got a big rush.

When I turned around, the camera guy and sport-top girl were glissading down and the rest of the party followed. I was hot, and I'm not referring to my temper. I took my helmet off, walked over to the stream, knelt down, and stuck my head right in the freezing glacial runoff. Whew! That was refreshing, but talk about brain freeze. Oddly, after I dipped my head in that freezing water my attitude improved some. Glacial runoff may have some special powers for hotheads like myself.

The hike out wasn't any shorter than the hike in — damn it! At the White River campground, Jenny rallied and appeared to be quite pleased with herself. She'd captured the summit of Rainier and lo and behold her husband had prepared a veritable feast complete with a glass of champagne for each of us to celebrate her.

There's no doubt in my mind that Jenny would've been happier if she'd simply been airlifted to the summit. I know I definitely would've been happier. With a climbing party that functioned as a flock of Sherpas, no climbing fees and a highly experienced lead climber Jenny should've felt like she was heading up to seventh heaven. Instead, she'd been a drag the entire time we climbed. If there's such a thing as "The Perfect Climb," that one sure wasn't it.

I had plenty of time to think about the way I acted on that climb, and my desire to change seemed pointless. I wasn't trying to win a popularity contest anyway, but I wanted a good alpine climb. I decided I'd try a new strategy — wiring my jaws shut before I went on a climb might work.

The following is my raw, unvarnished journal entry copied exactly as I wrote it. I suggest you buckle your seat belt because it isn't a nice trip.

### Mt. Rainier 2ᴺᴰ Summit July 2000

I have to say that going up the second time was better. Even though it was a new route, and I knew it would be different (harder too), I had a pretty good idea of what to expect based on last year. I didn't even know if I would get altitude sickness or not last year. I did get a headache at the summit this year, but I think it was because I hadn't slept for three nights in a row, and because I nearly ran up to Columbia Crest once we hit the crater rim. Moving fast at 14,411 feet isn't wise. I often had a hard time with our pace (it was slow most of the time), so I was better off at the end of our team of three. I did lead the descent from Camp Schurman to the trail at the base of the Interglacier and I tried to keep a slow pace. It was okay until about 300 feet from the bottom where I was very tired, and it was icy. I glissaded about 200 feet. I'm not sure what to do with my impatience. I want to reach the goal and when people stop to drink water and eat...I get irritable. When they move slowly... I get grumpy. I wanted to be better this year, but I found myself losing patience over and over again! Both times I summited with Cebe we were the last rope team down to the base camp. I woke up early and wanted to go. Cebe wanted to wait another hour or so to see if the wind would diminish. I told him I didn't think it would improve, but should just go anyway. We were the last party to depart the camp. This bothers me. Cebe let our team lead up to Camp Curtis and then down from Schurman. The heavy pack up to and down from Schurman kills my left shoulder (second degree separation... Due to injury 10 years ago). If I didn't have that problem...It would be impossible to go SO SLOW! My right knee (reconstructed 8 years ago) is swollen and hurts now. The descent hurt it. My left foot, with plantar fasciitis is sore too. The foot isn't as bad as the shoulder. The knee is also secondary to the shoulder. I need to get it fixed to be able to carry a pack weighing close to half my body weight for over 4 hours. I carried everything I needed plus a tent for 2, a rope, and a shovel. When Jenny almost gave up (before we hit snow) I took her parka, helmet and food. I carried all that clear up to Camp Curtis and my shoulder was almost numb, so I got others to take Jenny's gear. She does not belong on a glacial climb. She is too weak to just carry her essentials and NO GROUP GEAR! It pisses me off that she summited. She doesn't deserve a summit that she can't even carry her essential gear on. I will never climb with her again. She is slow and weak. I acted happy that she made it, celebrated with her and her husband, but I faked it. She never volunteered to help with our tent...I always had to prod her for help. She lent me toilet paper and dental floss and that's all she was good for. Harsh, huh? Why am I so judgmental? I know it's bad, but I can't help it. If I ever climb with Cebe again I will have to change my habit of voicing my thoughts and opinions. I am hardheaded and I wish I wasn't. That is mostly what I learned on this trip.

After I wrote that, I must've learned a few other things, because the next morning, I wrote this.

### GRAND TAHOMA

Wrapped in velvet blue, stars blaze across the sky.
This altitude is nothing, I just feel so high!
Twinkling lights snake up the corridor.
Tying in to the rope team my heart begins to soar.
Metal crampons crunching, ice ax in my hand,
headed to the summit, we begin to ascend.
Flash, then sputter of headlamp, sun begins to rise,
I'm now in heaven, it's spread before my eyes.
Crimson, gold, magenta, fill my every sense.

Peace and wonder in my heart, the beauty is intense.
Jumping ledge to ledge, over the crevasse,
endless cracks of aqua, more beautiful than glass.
Marvelous curves and angles, unknown to my eye,
appear below the ledge, as we go trudging by.
Sun cups across the snow, as far as I can see.
The sea of clouds below just fascinate me.
We summit grand Tahoma, she touches my soul.
Here at Columbia Crest, we have reached our goal.

Once my shoulder felt better, I doggedly returned to man shopping in Seattle. I'd never been a party girl, and the dating scene on Bainbridge Island was slim pickings for a woman in her forties, so if I didn't want to live alone for the rest of my life, I had to put myself out there. A few times each year I'd get dolled up, take the boat to the Emerald City and learn a few things about the men that inhabited it. The Queen City grill had the best decadent chocolate cake and a lot of horny old guys. The Oceanaire Restaurant had the best martinis and the biggest oyster bar in town, but the maitre'd was the only man who talked to me. Hanging out at a bar in an upscale restaurant was a bust. I'd just get hit on by drunk married men. No one could accuse me of sitting home alone darning socks, as I continued to party solo in Seattle.

Having no luck in classy establishments, I simply lowered my standards and hung out at bars where it was first come, first serve with fried food and loud music. I'd hit the Central and then The J&M Cafe and dance my butt off with a bunch of complete strangers and go up to Belltown to enjoy the music at the Crocodile. In Pioneer Square, I ventured into a couple of places. At Cowgirls Inc. I rode the mechanical bull in a room full of people that I would've sworn were teenagers with mixed drinks. I loved all the Irish pubs including The Owl and Thistle,

Fado and Kells. What I discovered was that all of those places had a lot of couples, and groups of men or women, but as a mature single shopper I was an outlier and never connected in a meaningful way with anyone over there. I eventually figured out that I was wasting my time and money and from that point on only went over to Seattle on a date.

I slowly came to the realization that since there were more men than women into mountaineering that my chances of meeting someone in the mountains were probably better than in bars. So far, I had zero luck meeting people in either environment but was cautiously optimistic. Since I was hell bent on climbing and would join almost any party that invited me up a mountainside, it was more likely that I'd meet the man of my dreams on a mountain. The upside of all that was that even if I didn't meet someone special while climbing, at least I'd buff up my climbing skills.

My client Sharon told me she'd gone out with a climber and they'd dated, but didn't click. She wanted to fix me up with him. I was glad she knew me well enough to set me up with a potential boyfriend/climbing partner, and that news was quite a pick-me-up.

# I LOVED CLIMBING IN CASHMERE

DICK MET ME for dinner at Moonfish, the most elegant restaurant on the island. I wore a form-fitting, low-cut black dress. I wanted the potential boyfriend to see that I was a real catch. The meal was off the chart good, Dick talked about himself and then covered a subject close to both of our hearts — climbing. He was older and had more climbing experience, especially in the Cascades Mountain Range. We planned a rock climb in the Cascades called South Early Winter Spire.

The chunk of rock we selected was the highest summit in the Liberty Bell group of the North Cascades. It's a three or four pitch climb, but Dick and I only used his rope twice on the way up when we climbed a chimney with a chock stone, and then again as I crossed an arete that Dick just walked across unroped. I didn't think we were doing anything unusual, because I felt comfortable mostly free soloing with him.

On the hike up, all at once we saw the huge spire rising up. Our destination looked closer than it really was, and it was slow going up to base through rocky rubble. I'd never been there before and Dick hadn't climbed it in quite a while, so we had to scout around to find the start of our climbing route. The first move was definitely the hardest, but then we cruised right on up. Shortly after we made that first tricky move, we passed a group of climbers who were placing shiny new pro. Their gear didn't have a scratch on it, which implied they were novices. I guess that's why they were roped up and going so slow. We ambled on by them unroped, and Dick told me they were probably Seattle Mountaineers. I asked him why he thought so.

"Their gear looks brand new, and they're roped together like they're scared to death." He said that deadpan, and I couldn't help laughing.

Eventually we came to a short chimney. I'd climbed some chimneys before, but nothing like this. It didn't go up very high, but it had a ceiling with the biggest chock stone I'd ever seen. I watched how Dick navigated up and around it, then tried it myself, and made it over the chock stone too.

We reached the top and had stellar views of Liberty Bell and a bunch of other peaks in the Cascades. We were alone up there, and the group we'd passed on the way up was nowhere in sight. Two climbers popped up on a northern route that's best described as a sheer drop off that encourages one to shout Geronimo before descending it. I wouldn't have attempted it unless I'd sent a copy of my living will to all my friends and family. Those two guys were worn out and sat down to rest. We asked them about their climb, and they told us they were from Canada and had their sights set on that difficult route for a while.

We bid them adieu and headed back down past the same group of slow moving roped climbers. They were about halfway up. As we passed them again, I couldn't make out what the instructor barked to his climbing party, but just like the Great and Powerful Oz, I'm sure their leader told them to pay no attention to us. We weren't roped and scampered down like a couple of mountain goats, as they tediously placed and removed trad gear.

We got back to Dick's car and stopped for gas. I bumped into Cebe at the gas station! He was leading a bunch of mountaineers up

Kangaroo Temple nearby. What a nice surprise to accidentally meet him in the mountains.

Then we went back to Dick's place. He had a gorgeous home with a view of the Cascade Mountains and plied me with food and drink. By then, I knew that we had no romantic future. Something was missing and there was no chance that sparks would fly, because when he talked to me I would've sworn I was being interrogated. I didn't know it at the time, but in a way I was.

Dick was very conservative and hard to talk to, and after my experience with Jake, I didn't trust my instincts. Dick tried to arrange another dinner date and I used that opportunity to tell him that I'd rather just climb with him. As soon as I said that he was ruffled. We'd been sitting on his sofa, and he stood up and brushed his sleeve as though wiping something unpleasant away. Then became agitated and went right into housekeeping mode as he tidied up the perfectly neat living room. After a few minutes of book straightening and magazine shuffling, I was sent packing.

Eventually I found out he'd been wife hunting, because when I called hoping to climb with him about 6 months later, the new wife answered and told me not to call back. Then I realized he hadn't been looking for a climbing partner. I'd apparently made the first cut, but was scratched off his list when I flatly fell on my face in the wife interview. So that was the end of that, but I had another potential climbing partner waiting in the wings who had no interest in sleeping with me.

My client Danielle was curious about rock climbing. She had some indoor climbing experience, so I took her up to Mission Creek Canyon near Cashmere, WA. Climbing there in the heat of summer was pleasant, because there were a lot of well-shaded climbing areas. We bouldered, did a couple of easy pitches on the rock walls, and then she was done. That was her first outdoor rock climb and I didn't want to push her, so we called it a day. As we were packing up to go, I met a couple, Kyle and Jan who were climbing there too. They asked me to join them there the following weekend.

I took Kyle and Jan up on their invite and went back to Cashmere. They were experienced rock climbers and *all* they did was trad climbing. They were both members of Olympic Mountain Rescue. I hoped to do some lead climbing, but we used most of our time and energy climbing one rock feature called "White Castle." That was a 5.7 plus and did have a couple of tricky spots. I was sloppy and punctured my right knee, but the injury was superficial.

After climbing some other routes that were top roped, we took a lunch break. Then we returned to a sunlit crack that faced out toward the road, and I'm sure I sprouted some gray hairs on that route! It had an easy 5.6 start, but then you'd go into a crack with an overhanging chock stone, and it got tough. Kyle just stemmed up and over the chock stone, but I had much shorter legs than him and couldn't do that. At about fifty feet up, I was worn out and afraid. I didn't know if I had the strength to go on.

When I managed to get over that damn stone and made it out of the crack, I got to a rest spot. After that, I took a long pull on my water bottle and caught my breath. I had to remove two pieces of pro on the boulder in front of me and do a lie back to get around it. First I tried to do a fist jam, but the crack was too small. I'd never done a lie back before, and was pretty sure I'd bitten off more than I could chew. A lie back is a technique used in cracks and corners. The legs push while the arms pull. It scared the living bejeezus out of me, but I pulled a couple times and came around to the other side of the boulder where Kyle had secured anchors.

We headed back to where we'd camped at the creek, and I couldn't wait to get all the grit off me and out of my navel piercing. I was thinking about going home, but the lure of new routes helped me to recover quickly. By the time I was clean, I'd changed my mind and wanted more.

You've probably guessed that creating a new route is much more interesting than climbing an established one. It was challenging too, but the challenges always charged me up. When the day was done, I was sore all through my shoulders, upper middle back and hips. My body was covered with cuts and scratches, I had bloody knuckles, and a nasty scab forming on my knee. I looked as if I'd been in a knock down drag out fight and lost, but I wasn't beaten. I only looked beat up because I had a blast!

Climbing in Cashmere required high octane fuel, so I ate an entire carton of Ben and Jerry's Cherry Garcia after I got home and flaked out. I had a good work week ahead and was thinking about heading back out to Cashmere in another week or two, because learning new climbing techniques turned me on!

The following weekend, Kyle hadn't called to tell me that he and Jan would meet me in Cashmere. I was pasting some rock climbing photos in my journal, when I decided to give my son Matt a call. He invited me to come visit him, and I drove to Port Townsend that afternoon. I thought about the rocky road we'd gone down. I think he blamed me for divorcing his dad, and decided that I was the bad guy who broke up our family, and there was some truth in that. Maybe he'd realized that his dad and I had some pretty big problems and couldn't stay married, but for whatever reason Matt and I got along fine now.

He'd gotten a small trailer and was living on the beach at Point Hudson. I was envious because I dreamed of doing that myself someday. Matt gave me a tour of the new place and his cat Felix took a liking to me. We went to Waterfront Pizza for a slice of the best pie in town and had a great time. He showed me his new tattoo, and I was jealous, because mine were much smaller. I told him that he could go rock climbing with me out near Anderson Lake. He said he would and launched into a story about his latest addiction, surfing. I asked him to join me on a beach walk, but he had other plans. I was just glad we'd had a chance to hang out together.

I drove out to North Beach to take that walk, parked my car, and headed west to "glass beach." The tide was low as I skirted the sandstone cliffs, and an eagle was fishing along the way. I stopped to watch a pair of eagles perched atop a towering Douglas fir tree up on the cliffs. One dived toward the water and captured a duck as the other ducks flapped, squawked and flew out of harm's way. The hunter brought the duck to the other eagle on top of the tree, who began to tear it apart. Feathers scattered in the wind.

Around the McCurdy Point where glass beach begins, the snow capped Olympic Mountains suddenly jumped up right in front of me. I stopped cold there on a long, lone stretch of sand dotted with glittering glass, and those gorgeous alpine mountains looked like I could reach out and touch them. While I collected bits of glass and pottery smoothed by tumbling in the waves, I could see more sparkling colored glass shining through wavelets that broke on the beach. When I'd visited the San Francisco Bay, the water there was an opaque coffee color, and I knew I was lucky to live in the Puget Sound region, because it's such a pristine part of the world. On the way back home, I decided to go to Cashmere the following weekend. If I couldn't join other climbers, scrambling was an option.

Cashmere was a school for me. I returned again and again that summer and fall and jumped at the chance to go there with Kyle and Jan. My skill level improved with practice, and I did my first leads with trad pro there. My truck bed with a camper shell made for comfortable sleeping into the fall, and I was glad I hadn't sold it and bought a motorcycle. Sometimes on Sundays, mountain bikers pedaled by, but no one was out there at night, and it was always peaceful and perfectly quiet.

I'd packed up and headed out of Mission Creek after a weekend of superb climbs and was driving home on Highway 2 with images of what I'd done floating through my head. I felt a rush just thinking about those climbs, plus it was such a beautiful drive. To top it all off, Kyle and Jan would be climbing Liberty Bell and invited me to join them! That chunk of rock was on *my* bucket list.

My climbing slate was full, and I couldn't have been happier, until I learned that Jake, my hellish ex-climbing partner, flummoxed the Liberty Bell climb for me. He would be a lead climber on that excursion and didn't want me in the climbing party. His personal vendetta was now spilling over into, and mucking up, my climbing plans. Any shred of regret I'd had about the end of our friendship went up in smoke, and all I wanted to do was put a rope around his neck and hang him from the tallest tree.

I didn't stay upset for long. Shortly after learning I couldn't climb the Liberty Bell, I was invited to return to Boulder to rock climb there with Scott. He was the man who'd taken the paper lining in my tin of mints on my second climb up Rainier.

After a couple of emails and a phone call or two, I decided to fly out to Denver and climb with him. He was an accomplished man, and his mountaineering resume included climbs from all over the world. He lived near so many wonderful sport and trad climbing areas that it sounded like he had the perfect life. Not only was he a top-notch climber, but he was well educated, attractive, and had a good career.

The first day I arrived, we headed out to climb. He was tall, with an athletic build, and talk about sexy! He really had it going on, and as he climbed the rock wall I studied his form with great interest. The area he took me to wasn't far from the road, and the rock formation was really jagged with huge chunks jutting out. It looked daunting to me. He flew right up, but when I tried to follow, my skill level didn't match his, and I had trouble negotiating it. I didn't ask, but wouldn't be surprised if my

John Wayne look-a-like climbed 5.12 or more based on what I saw him do over that weekend. I think he figured out right then and there on our first climb together what I was capable of, because the next day we did one of the best rock climbs ever.

He'd made it pretty clear that evening that he was interested in being more than my climbing partner. He only had one bedroom and that was in a loft. He offered to share his king sized bed with me, and I didn't even try to sleep on the sofa in his living room, because it looked so uncomfortable. I climbed into his big comfy bed and proceeded to spend most of the night fending him off. I'd scoot away when I felt his hands on me, but like an octopus he kept latching back on. I finally rolled over and told him that I barely knew him and would appreciate it if he'd let me get some sleep.

The next morning, we headed to El Dorado. Apparently that's a popular climbing spot for the locals, and it was too crowded. Then we went to the Flat Irons where I'd climbed the first Flat Iron with Jake. Scott picked a different route, on the third Flat Iron. It was all trad climbing too. We climbed six pitches to the summit of that massive rock formation, then did three rappels down the back side, and hiked out.

Normally, when you rappel, you don't want to go too fast. For one thing you want to stay in control and be able to stop whenever you need to. If the rope is too close to the rock wall, you might need to brake or at least slow down a lot to be able to push away from it with your legs. To preserve the integrity of the rope, you don't want to descend too rapidly because the outer sheath can be damaged by the heat generated from the metal ATC rubbing on the rope. Scott set up the rappel and I'd be the first one down. He explained that those were old ropes, and he was about to retire them, so I could use my own judgment on how fast I wanted to descend.

He'd given me the green light, and the rope wasn't anywhere near touching the wall. So I let myself practically fall down that rope. I flew down so fast that I could smell the fibers on the sheath singeing. I wondered if it was possible for the rope to catch fire, because if it could I'd soon be abseiling on a burning candlewick. It was such a blast that I couldn't decide which was more fun — climbing up or rappelling down! At the base of that climb, I was euphoric, and thought I must've skipped the light fandango (even though Fandango was the name of another route). I felt like I finally knew what that phrase meant in the song *Whiter Shade of Pale*.

I loved Boulder and imagined what a fabulous life I could have there. Scott might be the man I was looking for, with plenty of rope to spare, and I hoped he'd give me the slack I needed. I thought maybe we'd end up in a great relationship as a couple who loved to climb and loved each other. But he came on even stronger than before that evening and it was off putting. It rained all morning the next day, and I flew back to Seattle. We'd talked about climbing at Smith Rock sometime in the future. I was in love with Boulder, and if Scott would just slow down who knew what might happen.

After I got home we emailed back and forth and talked on the phone frequently. He decided to come out here and climb the Brothers with me, and I invited my friend Eddy to join us. The Brothers are easy to spot on the ferry from Seattle to Bainbridge Island. That mountain rises up and splits in two at the top. I see it every time I visit Cebe or my friend Lillith. It's smack dab in the middle of High School Road as you leave Safeway and head west.

Scott and I arrived at the trailhead to Lena Lake and met up with Eddy there. We hiked up past the lake and through a magical old growth forest called the Valley of the Silent Men. I expected to see Robin Hood or his band of merry men step out from behind one of the towering trees. A little further on we came to a spectacular wreck that was once a forest. A huge avalanche had flattened the woods. All that was left was an expanse that looked as if it had been blasted by explosives and what remained was a jumble of tree trunks crisscrossed and sometimes almost interlaced together. It reminded me of pickup sticks, except with huge trees. We had a good route map, but it didn't have *this* on it.

We threaded our way slowly through that mess. With heavy backpacks on we crawled over and under tree trunks and pulled ourselves through that wreck of the forest. There was no other way to get past it and it was tedious. I crawled under a tree and felt stuck. I pawed at the ground like a dog digging a hole as I tried to squeeze through there. It was a relief when Eddy unhooked my pack from a branch on that tree and freed me.

When we got to a rocky ridge top with no debris, we had to figure out where we were and how to get back on route. We tried to go one direction, but it was obviously the wrong way, and then tried to figure out how to climb from there, but that wouldn't work either. There was really only one other choice available, and once we went in that direction we found a cairn (a marker made from stacking stones). The cairn helped, but then we weren't sure how to get through the next wooded area. So far route finding was a bitch. We knew we were looking for a rock gully that would be above us somewhere to the west.

We entered woods that took us gradually higher and found the gully. Scrambling up the nearly vertical, dry gully filled with huge boulders chewed up a lot of our time. At the top, we didn't have much further to go. Once we arrived at the camping area, at 4,500 feet Scott chatted with a few other climbers to get more beta on the summit bid. We found a rocky, semi-flat area to set up our tents, and finding that site to pitch tents was our only reward after climbing that day.

We got up around 5:30 in the morning and started up toward the southern peak of the Brothers. After about 1,000 feet of kick-stepping up in the snow, the mountain was getting more and more icy. We roped up and used our ice axes. There were two other climbing parties below us, and we saw them pack up and leave. I thought that was odd, because the night before they'd told Scott they'd attempt the summit around the same time we did.

Eddy suggested we pack it in, too, and do it another time, but I was adamant about reaching the top. Scott said we could make it if we cut steps in the ice. I didn't know the first thing about cutting steps in the ice, but was eager to do it. Scott and I won out at last when Eddy said okay. We took turns cutting steps, and that took us an hour and a half to climb under 1,000 feet to the summit of the southern peak. I could've crawled there faster if it hadn't been so icy. That was the first and last time I'd be enthusiastic about cutting steps on an icy mountain top.

At the summit we saw patches of blue sky appear through big, puffy, white clouds swirling around us. The north peak was close by, and we talked about traversing from one peak to the other. I still hadn't done a traverse from peak to peak and that one looked intimidating. We all got the summit pictures we wanted and headed back down.

Eddy and Scott merrily plunge-stepped down the steep slope from the summit jabbering away, while I was so beat after cutting steps in the ice that I could barely break the crust on the snow in my crampons. My progress down that snow-covered mountain resembled someone who'd just gotten off an amusement park ride and was dizzy. I was more or less zig-zagging down the slope and then my boot would slip out from underneath me, and I'd stab the snow with my ice axe and land on my butt. The guys didn't notice I was having trouble because I didn't yell "Falling." I knew I'd be able to stop myself, until one time I almost slammed into them, and they gave me holy hell for not alerting them."

I explained that I was thrashed and couldn't help it, and I was more or less slip-sliding down the mountain. After paying attention to my flailing efforts for a couple minutes, they seemed satisfied that what I was doing was more like taking a step or two and then just sitting down hard. So they continued their banter and romped on downhill oblivious to me, while I sweated out my descent attempting to stay upright.

That was one of the most physically difficult climbs I'd done. On that descent I was a mess, as I stepped, slipped and plopped down. I wished I'd listened to Eddy and vowed never to do anything like that again. It was harder than climbing Mt. Rainier. I don't even know if we would've found the high camp if Eddy hadn't been with us. He'd summited the Brothers before, and since he was familiar with the terrain was able to get us back on track when we were floundering.

Finally we got back down in the Valley of the Silent Men. One of those silent men must've had it in for me, because as I stepped on a thick, wet, slippery bed of pine needles my ankle folded sharply to one side. I glanced at it and thought, "Ankles aren't supposed to bend like that." Then I really took a hard look at it and knew I was in big trouble. The guys were immediately at my side. Big Eddy picked me up and like a little toy and tried to get me on my feet. I put weight on my left ankle for just an instant and sat right back down, because it was excruciatingly painful.

We were about five miles from the cars. It would've been so humiliating to make Mountain Rescue come pick me up, because I twisted my ankle. I now wish I had let them carry me out, because to this day that ankle gives me trouble. I asked Eddy what I should do. He wondered if I had a compression wrap and thank god I did. He wrapped my already swelling ankle snugly and nearly emptied my pack into his, then asked me to try to walk. I could, but it hurt like hell as I hobbled down the trail.

Scott filled his pack with some of my stuff too and we kept going. I wasn't sure if I could make it out of the woods (literally), but of course I did. Later that evening, Scott wanted to know where we stood, and I told him I liked everything about him, but as far as a relationship went my heart wasn't in it. If I'd told him everything I was thinking about, things might have turned out differently. The good news was that Eddy had a good time.

It took 2 months before I could run pain free. My ankle injury should've been treated by a doctor. Call me vain, but I didn't want to stomp around in a moon boot and simply waited until it healed on its own.

When my ankle felt much better, I flew back east to visit my dad. When I was in junior high school, I'd been placed in the California State Gifted Program and won presidential physical fitness awards three years in a row. I'd wondered for years why he and my mom had never helped or encouraged me to get into sports or go to college.

On that visit, Dad answered those questions without provocation. He told me he hadn't gone to college and had done fine. He said he didn't know why everyone thought college was so important. Then he looked at me and said, "You were such a pretty little girl, and I knew one day you'd meet a nice man who'd take good care of you." I was flabbergasted. At that time I was in my forties, and that nice man hadn't materialized. I didn't respond, but was thinking, *Where the hell is that damn Prince Charming?*

When I got home from that trip, I began to think about joining the Seattle Mountaineers Club. Finding regular climbing partners was about as much fun as searching for a contact lens on the beach. Cebe was busy teaching classes and writing for the club, so he hadn't climbed with me lately. Since Jake and I were history, I needed more climbing buddies and I figured joining the Mountaineers might solve that problem.

# THE MOUNTAINEERS AND MY SWEET CLIMBING SISTER

||||||||||||||||||||||||||||||||||||||||||||||||||||||||||||||||||||||||||||||||||||||||||||||||||||||||||||||||||||||

I LOOKED INTO how the Seattle Mountaineers Club worked. If I took the basic climbing course, when I finished it I'd have many climbs to choose from and never have to worry about finding a climbing partner again. That would be ideal, so I plunked down the money and waited for the course to begin. I managed to do some rock climbing but still hoped for a regular partner.

When the classes began, I was already a fairly good climber, so the course wasn't a challenge for me, but I got a mean-spirited feeling about the club right out of the gate. In the knot tying class I'd learned how to tie knots I'd never heard of before and had no idea what practical use they might serve. I practiced them all over and over and had no trouble showing the instructors how to tie them correctly. After everyone demonstrated their skills, one of the teachers gave a talk about belaying, and explained how to use the figure eight knot to do that.

I found that portion of the class really boring and was daydreaming about some of the more unusual ways I'd belayed. I recalled one time when the lead climber tied me in from the back. That was probably the most comfortable belay I'd ever done. I raised my hand and when

I was called on I described that. The instructor cut me off mid-sentence and jumped down my throat. He looked like he was about to have a stroke. "Mountaineers never do that because it's dangerous!" I wanted to counter that by saying the lead climber was an expert. The teacher didn't give me a chance to say anything and said, "We need to be able to see that we are all using the correct knots."

I thought, *How stupid!* If you know your partner and their skill level, what's the problem? I'd spent hours and hours learning knots that I would never use. Most of the time the figure eight was all I needed, and I wondered who the hell decided that we needed to learn so many other stupid knots. That instructor verbally flogged me in front of about thirty people, and I wondered how much more unnecessary crap like that I'd have to put up with.

I talked to Cebe about the knot class, and he pointed out that usually you don't know your partners, so having standard practices made it easy to see if everyone is safe. That made sense, but that man's attitude didn't.

The navigation course was fun. They took us into the mountains and tried to get us lost. We used our maps and compasses to find our way out, and it was a big game. As we walked back down to the cars, I was describing my nude summit on Mt. Rainier to a handsome club member who'd just told me he was a pilot. A guy directly in front of us, stopped in his tracks and turned to face me.

"*You* did that? I thought it was just a story." I assured him that I was real and actually did strip naked on the summit. Later I gave that exchange some thought and was surprised that my nude photo shoot on Rainier had achieved something akin to legendary status.

In the next class we climbed a concrete structure to practice rock climbing moves. I thought, "What a joke. They want us to demonstrate rappelling on that?" The structure might have been all of 20 feet tall and we had to rappel off it. I did everything they wanted and rappelled off that lame fake rock, but was pretty disgusted with the whole program by then. That class didn't seem realistic to me at all. I really didn't want to climb with anyone who thought they had climbing skills based on an experience like that, and I quit. The one class I'd been looking forward to was crevasse rescue, because I hadn't done that in real life, but my short fuse got the better of me.

Shortly after I dropped out of the Seattle Mountaineers, I overheard some guys on the ferry talking about them. I moved closer and opened my book. I had to repress a giggle when they said you could spot them a mile away with all their shiny new gear. My mind bounced right back to that climb with Dick and the Great and Powerful Oz. It would've been nice to have a lot of climbing partners, but I actually wanted to climb with people I knew and trusted.

After the mountaineers fiasco, I met Jilly. We had a friend in common who encouraged us to meet. She was tall and leggy, with short auburn hair and dark chocolate brown eyes. I thought she'd be able to make amazing moves with her long limbs.

Jilly glowed with a healthy tan and appeared to be the outdoorsy type dressed in a sports top, sage green capri tights and an old pair of beat up sneakers. But after we talked she struck me as a gentlewoman with her soft voice and graceful mannerisms, disguised as an outdoors-woman. We exchanged contact information and I suggested we try meeting at the indoor gym in Bremerton. I had plans for outdoor climbs soon and we could do that if she wanted to. She liked my ideas and invited me to hike with her. I thought we'd be a good team. We went on a few hikes in the state forest with her dog, a brown and white cocker spaniel named Ginger. I generally liked dogs, but that one didn't respond to commands and Jilly wouldn't put a leash on it.

Shortly after I met her, the stars must have been in alignment, because a big man with penetrating azure blue eyes introduced himself and wanted me to be his personal trainer. Clint was heavyset and wanted my help to get in better shape. He fit neatly into my early morning time slot, so I scheduled him in.

After a run at the track, he said he was going to Kingston for dinner and wondered if I'd join him. I explained that I didn't date clients, and he pointed out that he'd go with or without me, but if I joined him we'd have a good meal and could talk about his training plan. Then he insisted that it wasn't a date. I'd enjoyed his company so much that I decided to bend the rules.

He took me to the Kingston Ale House on a big Harley road bike that evening. I discovered his delightfully candid sense of humor that bordered on raunchy and caught me off guard. Several times he made me laugh so hard that my stomach hurt. We spent that evening talking about everything except his workouts. The Harley ride and his winning personality were pure fun, and I hoped we'd get together again soon.

Jilly and I decided to climb at Frenchman Coulee. As we scouted for our first climb I told her that I'd met a potential boyfriend and she said, "That's nice" and promptly changed the subject. As we scanned the Sunshine Wall I swung around to face her and my gear clanked on the sling. I wanted to get a read on her. She had a bored expression, and I was surprised that she wasn't happy for me.

Who did I run into there but Jake? I'd avoided him like the plague and no longer hiked with his outdoor club. I also quizzed climbing parties about who was on their climb. Unfortunately, the people I knew and wanted to climb with in that camping area were his friends too. Jilly had taken off with Ginger to inspect the Feathers when I spotted him. I knew I'd have to acknowledge his presence at some point, but all I really wanted to do was kick him where it counts.

Ever the good actor, he walked right over to me and said, "So Paula, how are things?" None of his buddies were near me. It was the perfect opportunity to give him a piece of my mind. Instead, I didn't say a word to him and just turned and walked away. Later I thought I should've said, "Blowing me off the Liberty Bell was as low as you could go. Go blow yourself." Of course hindsight is 20/20, but I didn't need to spell it out, because actions do speak louder than words and I'm sure he got the message. Then the clouds burst and dumped rain on us. Slogging around in the mud isn't my idea of a good time, and Jilly agreed. We drove home and I never saw Jake again.

When the weather took a turn for the better, Jilly took me on a hike up to a mountain lake in the Cascades. It was hot and sunny that day, so when we arrived at that lake I was soaked with sweat. The only people in sight were far away on the opposite shore and I hadn't heard anyone behind us on the trail. I stripped down and told Jilly to join me for a swim. She was reluctant, and I went on in butt naked. The water was shockingly cold, but felt refreshing at first.

Jilly undressed, waded in and we had a water fight. I splashed her furiously then she disappeared underwater. I decided to swim underwater too and then get out. I popped up facing the opposite shore and stood thigh deep in the lake when I thought I heard someone behind me. I turned and saw a man, a boy, and a woman who was pointing to our clothes. I locked eyes with that woman and then went back underwater. When I resurfaced near Jilly, we were both neck deep in the lake and she whispered, "There's a family standing right over there watching us like zoo animals." I hoped those people would leave soon because my teeth were beginning to chatter, and I wondered where the hell Ginger was. That dog's only talent seemed to be aggressively scaring the hell out of people, but the one time I could've used her greatest skill, she was nowhere in sight.

I couldn't hear exactly what they said, but the woman grabbed the kid's hand and they all walked back to the trail. The boy looked back at us over his shoulder a couple times and each time he did the woman yanked on him so hard I thought she would dislocate his shoulder as she shook him. Once they'd gone we didn't bother to dry off and struggled to get our clothes on. We had a good laugh about the hikers who'd found us naked.

Later a few days after that hike, I was kicked back in the sky chair on the deck of my apartment, reflecting on the lake hike and was pretty sure that we hadn't damaged that boy's psyche. I knew he'd see worse things in life than two naked ladies cavorting in a lake, and it was possible that his dad might take him on more hikes based on that episode.

I wasn't expecting anyone and wasn't playing my stereo, so when someone knocked at the door, I wondered who it could be. My loud music was usually the only reason I'd get a knock on the door. When I opened it, I saw Chance. He was taking me up on my offer of a beer. I got two quart-size galvanized steel buckets, filled them with ice and jammed bottles of IPA in both. He was out on my deck admiring the view of the harbor, and I handed him my church key and set the buckets on the table. He popped the tops and we began to learn more about each other.

I gave him the low down on my personal training and told him I was into climbing. He was working for congressman Jay Inslee and had a cool cat named Tuxedo. Then he asked me if I knew about the history of the Japanese on Bainbridge island. I didn't know anything about it. He said that during World War II the Japanese were rounded up and sent to concentration camps. I was horrified and said, "That's unthinkable." Chance nodded, and said a lot of people in our country didn't know what happened to Japanese-Americans in World War II, because it was swept under the rug. The dock where the Japanese were shuttled onto boats like cattle no longer existed, but there was hope of purchasing that land and building a memorial to commemorate that infamous event. Chance worked on that and helped to make it a reality years later.

He wondered if I wanted to go kayaking with him in a week or two. I told him honestly, it was prime time for climbing and a miracle that he'd found me at home. He laughed and we had another brew and clinked bottles toasting the perfect weather.

Climbing with Kyle and Jan a week later in Mission Creek Canyon it was another cloudy day. Not a ray of sun made its way down into the canyon, but the temperature was fine. There were good spots to place anchors with an easy walk off. I belayed Kyle, and we got soaked in a torrential downpour. I packed up and told Jan and Kyle that I'd come back when it looked like we didn't need to board the ark.

The following weekend Jilly, Clint and I joined Kyle in Mission Creek Canyon. Clint learned to belay with no trouble. He didn't want to climb, but enjoyed being a part of the team. I had a good time leading a couple of 5.8's and Jilly cleaned (removed my pro as she climbed up).

I asked Jilly to practice crevasse rescue with me. I thought we'd be able to summit any peak if I could teach her a few more skills. She wasn't interested and let me know that she was more than satisfied with her current skill level.

Whenever I spent time with Jilly, I had to remind myself not to offend her. She had this thing about her dog. If anyone said something she didn't like about Ginger, they ended up in the doghouse. I'd discovered that she was the sensitive type and I had to keep my mouth shut on various topics that might upset her. She was planning to throw a summer solstice party in the community center at her apartment complex and invited me. I asked if I could bring my oldest son, and she said no kids were allowed. I thought she was being mean, because she knew he was over 18, but I smiled and all I said was, "Okay Jilly."

I usually agreed to do anything she suggested and didn't balk if she declined my invitations or training suggestions, and that as you must know by now, was a considerable concession for me. I wondered if she would ever want to lead on rock routes, and become a more proficient climbing partner. I'd have to just wait and see on that score. It had taken me a long time to find her, and I really didn't want to lose her by pushing too hard.

After a few more hikes I took Jilly up to Valhalla, which was a new experience for her. She was thrilled when we got up there. That rocky crag is located in a place that provides an amazing 360 degree view in the Olympics. To the left we saw Mt. Constance from a truly unique angle above the approach to it and Mt Baker far away in the Cascades. Directly in front of us we looked down across the forested hills to the Hood Canal and over to the Cascades where Mt. Rainier was crowned with a lenticular cap floating around her top. To the right we saw Mt. Jupiter and the Brothers with the interior of the national park spreading out behind us. She softly said, "Thank you" as she slowly turned to drink it all in. I don't know why I never snapped a picture of her, she was a real beauty.

For some reason, we never met at restaurants, went to the movies or did anything that friends normally do together. It was as if I had an adventure contract with her and friendship wasn't penned in. I wasn't okay with that. I wanted to get to know her better and share some leisure time. When I saw her in the gym every once in a blue moon, she didn't like me to interrupt her routine.

I walked into the locker room of the gym at 5:45 one morning, to look for a client and noticed almost everyone was transfixed and staring up at the TV screens. I saw a plane fly into a tall building and thought it was a movie. All the women were behaving as though it was real, and the entire room resounded with the sharp intake of breath!

I looked at the TV again and saw that the buildings were the twin towers in New York, and it was being broadcast on CNN. I asked the woman next to me "What's going on?" She said she wasn't sure but what we were seeing was real. The TVs in the gym had no sound. Later that day, I learned the horrifying details and felt a lot of anxiety. The effect of witnessing that terrorist attack is hard to describe. I wasn't able to work, because I couldn't concentrate, and my clients were also a complete mess. I spent the remainder of that day in the safety of my home in an attempt to diffuse my fear and anxiety.

Later Jilly and I talked about the horrible tragedy, and we both felt powerless. She was confused, but I was upset. She hoped the government would find a way to solve the problem with the terrorists. I had my doubts about that. In 1980 I was in boot camp, and we'd been primed to go to the Middle East, but never did. I often wonder how our presence there might've reshaped the future, but I didn't share that thought with Jilly or anyone else.

I'd stayed in touch with Jean, one of the Canadians from Red Rocks. He came down from Canada to visit friends in Seattle and we arranged to climb together. When he arrived, after some prodding he admitted that the only outdoor climbing he'd done was at Red Rocks! I had a spare bedroom, so I put him up for a couple nights.

Jilly came up with the idea of climbing trad with him. I was totally surprised since she never seemed to want to climb with anyone except me. I thought about the boat trip Clint had invited Jilly on. All three of us had gone to Blake Island including the dog two months before, and she'd never suggested that Clint join us.

She wanted to explore Little Si with Jean and me. Of course, we wanted to go. Mount Si is a mountain that's been seen by anyone who watched the TV show *Twin Peaks*. On the west side, there's a class three scramble up to the Haystack (the top), but we went around to the back of the mountain, on the east side to rock climb. Scrambling is much like hiking, but you need to use your hands sometimes and we wanted to use our hands to climb.

When we got to the first climbing area, we all stood around and stared at what we assumed was the rock wall that we'd climb. We were in the middle of a densely wooded area and that wall shot straight up in front of us. It was dimly lit in the mossy climbing area, and I couldn't see any bolts to clip into. I asked Jilly if she saw a way up and we all started looking around hoping we'd see something that indicated we were at the right spot. If we were, it would be purely trad climbing, because there weren't any bolts on the rock walls.

I'd have to place all the pro on any routes we climbed. I used to want to do that, but my feelings were beginning to change. Neither of them could lead and I might have to do some hard work placing protection on the route so they could climb. If Jilly could swing leads with me, I would have felt completely different.

I'd only fallen and kissed the wall once on lead when I was tired, and I had no desire to do that again. When I peeled off that rock wall, my helmet smacked into it and gave me a blistering headache. Hoping for anchors, I suggested we hike up and look around.

We went up a brush-filled gully and found the top of the rock wall. It must've been my lucky day, because I found anchors, and told Jilly I'd rappel down, and she could follow. I pulled the rope out of my rope bag, when Jilly said she'd never rappelled before.

I was shocked and dropped the rope while I stared at her. She'd often told me about climbing nine-thousand-foot peaks in the Cascades and described trad climbs she'd done. I was just beginning to realize the full extent of her lack of skill, and thought she must like to brag.

She'd apparently tagged along with climbers who allowed her to follow, and I was just another one of those people. She didn't own a rope or any climbing pro and was truly a hanger-on. No good could come from being too judgy about that though, and I reminded myself that she was a woman close to my age, who liked to climb, and that such a woman was a rare find. Still, she really needed to learn to rappel if she planned on doing much more climbing with me. I managed to talk her into it, but not Jean.

We all climbed that route and had a good time. Then I went back up and put the rope through the next set of anchors. That route was more difficult than the first, and Jilly with those long, beautiful legs was able to climb up further than I could.

While we were doing one last climb on another route, we noticed a man taking pictures of us. I was on lead and really didn't care what they were doing down there. As I leaned into the rock studying what I hoped was my next move, Jilly yelled up, "*Send it, Paula!*" That was the nudge I needed, so I took a chance and dynoed (jumped) to next position on the route. Then this guy yelled up, and asked if he could take some pictures of me climbing. I shouted back, "Sure!"

When I came down, he was still there and wanted to know if he could use the photos in a climbing book he was working on. I said be my guest. I asked if he knew what the route I'd just done was rated. He told me that it was a 5.10! After that, I took a couple pictures of Jilly, and she took a few of me.

On the way home, I thought again what a help it would be if Jilly could lead. She didn't have trouble learning to rappel, but I'd have to wait until we were alone, and she was in a receptive mood to suggest lead climbing. Jean packed up to go home, and I didn't want to climb with him anymore. I kept his contact information because I wanted to climb in Canada. He thanked me as he left. Who knows — maybe he'd bust out of the gym and try climbing outside again after our weekend together.

I told Clint about rock climbing at Little Si, and he was familiar with the area. During dinner on his boat, we talked about hiking up to the Haystack — just the two of us. After that meal he invited me to go on a motorcycle trip to Soap Lake. I'd been wondering when our relationship was going to the next level.

# YOU CAN PLEASE SOME OF THE PEOPLE SOME OF THE TIME

CLINT SAID RIDING out to Soap Lake was a weekend-long trip, and I knew what that meant. I had to decide if I wanted to do more than kiss him. He was a complete gentleman and hadn't put any pressure on me for sex. I cared about him, but wasn't in love. He'd dropped 25 pounds and looked pretty damn good to me. I'd wondered if we were physically compatible and said, "I'd love to go." We decided to go that Friday afternoon. It turned out to be a wonderful sightseeing tour and we had no problems in the bedroom.

I invited Jilly to join me at Steeple Rock on Hurricane Ridge, right after I got back from Soap Lake. She wanted to bring her friend Phoebe along. I asked if Phoebe had any experience rock climbing or scrambling and Jilly said she did, so I said okay. We decided to go in my truck, because I had a king cab and we'd all fit.

I drove over to Jilly's place and noticed she was wearing the Julbo Glacier glasses I'd given her. I didn't like the way they fit me. I picked her up with Phoebe who'd apparently spent the night there in Jilly's tiny, studio apartment and I wondered where her friend had slept. I looked around and Phoebe was in the bathroom. "Where'd Phoebe sleep last night?"

"She climbed in bed with me and we snuggled."

" Uh huh."

Ginger had to stay at home that day. Oh darn! You can't take dogs into the national park, and we'd be close to the ranger's office by the lodge too. As we hiked to Steeple Rock, I felt like a third wheel, because Jilly and Phoebe were so palsy-walsy. They looked like an adorable couple as they walked hand in hand seeming to prefer being alone together.

I led quite a distance ahead of them. I realized no one had a map. I'd read the description of the route the night before in my *Olympic Climbing Guide*, but somehow managed to forget the book and couldn't remember where to start. Jilly picked out a ridge on the northeast side. It looked doable and we scrambled up.

Eventually we got into a jam and I could see that we needed a rope to continue safely, so we all descended slowly. The miracle of miracles was that I remembered to bring a camera and took pictures of the great views from Port Angeles and the Straits of Juan de Fuca all the way over to Mt. Baker. Once I got home, I picked up the book that I should've brought. We'd been on a route that required a rope and belaying. I was glad I'd turned us around when I did.

I bumped into Jilly at the gym after our Steeple Rock adventure. She was nearly bursting at the seams with excitement and told me she'd bought a lot in eastern Washington. She told me about her plans to build a cabin and move there. This was all an unexpected news flash for me. She'd never mentioned the very idea of buying land, or moving.

Her property was about six hours by car from the Island. I began to wonder if she was independently wealthy, because I had no idea how anyone could make a living out there. She told me we should climb there. I'd never been there, but wanted to go. She had an old VW bus and decided it would be more comfortable than her jeep or my truck.

We took off on a hot, sunny day and passed through the Seattle area. The traffic was heavy as we crawled north on Interstate 5 with the windows down. We spotted a car with two handsome men who were obviously studying us too. They pulled up beside us and let Jilly know in no uncertain terms that they'd like us to flash them. Jilly and I had nothing to be ashamed of, but agreed it was pointless.

When we got into the mountains, the VW bus chugged slowly uphill, and I wished we'd taken my truck. Cars whizzed by us and I said something about crawling uphill. Jilly didn't respond and acted as if she hadn't heard me, so I dropped that subject.

As we neared our destination she suggested we rock climb first, and then head back to her property later. I thought that sounded fine. The problem was we had no idea where the climbing areas were. We stopped at the Goat's Beard, a local climbing supply store, and asked around. The clerks in the store didn't know diddly about it.

Heading out the door I bumped into Sean. I'd met him on a climb with Cebe. He was a good-looking man about ten years younger than me, and a skilled climber. We chatted briefly and I met his beautiful climbing partner, Sarah. He knew how to get to the climbing areas nearby and gave clear instructions on how to find them.

We started out at Fun Rock. There wasn't anyone there. It was a hot, dry summer and scrub brush abounded. Sean had only told us how to get there, and I wondered how much fun this rock would actually be.

Whether it was fun or not we looked great. I was wearing my new mint green Patagonia capris and matching top with a pair of sea green Black Diamond climbing shoes. Jilly could have worn a burlap sack and still look great, but she had on cute duds too.

I started up the first route I saw and used my quick draws (a pair of carabiners connected by a short sling). I was about 25 feet up the wall when Jilly said, "Hey, do you hear that?" Her dog had been restless because of the long ride in the bus and was running around barking non-stop. I couldn't hear much because Ginger was going off, but in between woofs I heard the distinct sound of a water sprinkler and thought, *Huh, that sounds familiar.* I'd heard that when I was a kid on my grandfather's ranch in Porterville, California.

"Jilly, get that dog up here right now. It's a rattlesnake!"

She called the dog to her side and helped belay me down off the rock. That rattler was really close by and I kept hearing it intermittently on my way down. With that in mind, I probably would've been better off climbing up, but I didn't want Jilly to get hurt. On the other hand, I'd sooner be rid of that damn dog. I unclipped two quick draws, and then we were out of there so fast it would make your head spin. We couldn't go back the way we came in because the huge snake was blocking the way.

Something I appreciated about Jilly was a quality I wished I'd had. She was able to just relax into a moment and completely change gears. She possessed a tranquility I had no access to. I was gripped with anxiety and said to her, "What should we do now? Will we go back to the car? Should we try to find the other climbing area?" She calmly said, "Why don't we just hike along here and see what else there is." That never would've occurred to me. I was jittery from the snake escape. She wasn't ruffled at all, and we moseyed along the dry trail that was parallel to the road.

We found a small group of men rock climbing, and for the first time Ginger didn't bark at the strangers. That climbing area wasn't as open as the one we'd left and was surrounded by tall trees. The rock wall had quite a ceiling about ¾ of the way up, and looked less challenging after that. We stood around and watched for a while and chatted with the other climbers. The man I'd first seen moving across that ceiling was a tall, lanky blond. His build was similar to Jilly's.

We asked them what that climb was rated, and they told us it was mostly 5.8, but had one tough move that was probably a 5.10. Jilly and

I had only done a 5.10 once by accident. We started to look for another route, but those guys were very encouraging and urged us to try it, because they were done climbing there.

I decided to give it a go, so one of the other climbers belayed me and two others stayed to watch. Jilly didn't want to do it. I did fine until I got to the overhang, and I guess that was the 5.10 move. I'd really studied how the tall guy did it, but once I got there, I was too short to repeat his moves. Poised clinging to the rock I thought I might get above it more directly but was hesitant to try a different way. Jilly shouted the magic words, "Send it!" When I heard her urging me on, I managed to navigate my way up and over the roof.

I wish I had a tape recording of her shouting "Send it, Paula!" I could just play that tape over and over and get all manner of things done! The guys below literally hooted and howled like animals. I would've sworn that there was an excited chimpanzee down there as I found a way up to the top of that route. I got quite a reception and looked down to see the tall blond man making those wild chimp noises. When I descended, they clapped me on the back and gave me huge kudos. One of them actually congratulated me on finding a new way to do the route. It was a huge dose of positive feedback.

I'd seen the walk-off from the top of the route, so top roped another route that looked pretty easy for Jilly. It could have been a 5.6 or 5.7, but I didn't want to climb it, because it didn't interest me. I belayed Jilly as she climbed up and she had a good time. By then, it was beginning to get dark. We decided to pack up and go find her lot. When we were walking out, there was no sign of rattlesnakes.

Jilly drove us up to her land and showed me the perimeters. It was small, but she could build a sweet little cabin there. We cleaned up as best we could and went into Winthrop, a nearby town that had restaurants. We were thinking of having dinner and a beer.

The place we chose in Winthrop was jam packed. There'd been some kind of music festival there that day, and we noticed a row of six motorcycles. They were all top-of-the-line late model bikes and could've been an advertisement for Ducati. We stood around inside the restaurant for a while, and then a good-looking older man walked over and asked if we'd like to join him and his friends. We looked at each other, smiled, and said yes.

We were led to a big, oval wooden table out on the back deck. That dining area was well-lit with party lights, and rock music was playing. It was a madhouse with other large tables full of people who were laughing and talking loudly over the music. Waitresses were practically banging into each other in an attempt to deliver drinks. I sat down, and Jilly was on the other side of me next to the man who led us over. Those guys had four other friends there with them and even though it was a table for six, they managed to squeeze us little climbing gals in.

We had dinner and drinks. I enjoyed their company and was sitting next to Chuck who was easy to talk to. He and his buddies had come down from Canada on their motorcycles for the music festival and would be returning the next day. We tried to pay our bill, but the Canadians beat us to it. I wondered why we didn't have gentlemen of their caliber where I lived.

Later on that evening there was a peculiar chemical smell in the air. I asked Jilly about it, and I can't remember her explanation, but I think it had something to do with a neighbor. We could've stayed another day and done more climbs, but she wanted to leave.

On the way home, Jilly was unnaturally quiet and that's always a bad sign. There was a trail she wanted to hike, and I wanted to join her. It was in the Cascade National Park, and her dog was off-leash as always. Jilly had recently broken up with Phoebe because of something she said about Ginger. So I bit my lip again and said nothing about the dog.

On this hike Ginger scared the shit out of some people on the trail, and they asked me why *my* dog was off-leash, and said the dog growled and bared its teeth at them. They were angry with me, so I explained it was my friend's dog and told them I was sorry. When Jilly caught up with me, I told her what those people had said, and her only response was an icy cold look. I decided to tell her the truth and finally told her in no uncertain terms, what I thought about her dog. She didn't say a word to me the rest of the way home.

When Jilly had told me about her dream of building a cabin, and we'd made a plan to climb near there, I'd explained that I was going to study for a big exam after we came back. I wouldn't be able to do any climbing for at least a couple months while I crammed for the big tests. So, I wasn't surprised when I didn't hear from her for a while after that weekend on her property.

Climbing had to go on the back burner for me then, because I had to study for an exam to be certified by the American College of Sports Medicine. The ACSM encourages people to get a two-year associates degree in exercise science before taking the test. I didn't have a college education, so I had to submit a petition to take the test. With ten years of experience in the field I was invited to take the written and practical exams. There were a couple of top-notch health clubs in Seattle that required that certification and I was considering working in one part-time.

After six weeks of study, I needed to get my nose out of the books for a day or two. Clint had the perfect solution. We went to the Oyster Run in Anacortes. That was the first motorcycle rally I'd been to, and it was a huge party. The streets were packed with bikes. We saw unique vintage motorcycles, gorged on oysters, and spent the night in a motel. It was a terrific weekend and a much needed break from my studies.

Jilly gave me a call shortly after I got back from the Oyster Run. I gave her the run down on my trip and she sounded irritated on the phone.

About a week after that call, I got a Dear Jane letter and Jilly kicked me to the curb. I was accused of chastising her for letting her dog off-leash, complaining about her VW van being slow, telling her I was going to do nothing but study, and then spent a weekend out of town with Clint. And those were only three of ten upsetting items she'd complained about.

I sat down and carefully considered her letter and replied. I apologized and tried to explain my behavior. I'd written a short story that featured her and enclosed it with my letter. She never replied, and I was confused and hurt, because I can usually figure out when I've committed an unforgivable sin, and the problems she'd illustrated could have been solved during a calm discussion or even a heated one.

During the cross-country trip when my family moved from California to Virginia, I was 14 years old, riding in the back of the station wagon absorbed in reading *Stranger in a Strange Land* and wished I knew more about grok. In that book *grok* means *understand*. Well, I sure didn't understand why my parents were jerking us into the middle of nowhere. I didn't grok the loss of my good friend Jilly either. Losing her friendship was upsetting. Without her the landscape had changed, but I knew I'd make new friends and find new climbing partners.

Jilly was a beautiful climber and had a lot of qualities I admired. My abrasive personality must have rubbed her the wrong way one, or even ten times too many. I'd made a bigger effort to be considerate of her than I had with anyone else before in my life. After giving the Jilly problem more thought, the reality of what I took to be a friendship struck me as something different.

Actually we were strangers who occasionally hiked or rock climbed and as a result much of what we said to each other was lost in translation. I felt as if she'd toyed with me, because connecting with her was like trying to hit a piñata just out of my reach. For whatever reason, Jilly hadn't allowed me to get close to her, and I was sorry she threw the towel in.

After I passed the ACSM tests, I was still climbing with Kyle and Jan, and Kyle surprised me while we were rock climbing one day when he suggested I join mountain rescue. I knew he and Jan were members, and asked him if he thought I was eligible. He told me that, with my glacier experience and rock climbing ability, that I had reasonable entry level skill. If I joined, I'd be able to do rescue missions after completing their training program.

Although I'd done well in the Army, I wasn't sure I wanted to be involved in another male-dominated organization. I took some time to digest the idea of joining mountain rescue, then finally wrapped my head around it. In addition to performing rescue missions, I thought I might find some new climbing partners too. I was curious, and asked Kyle how to join. It wasn't a military organization, but I saw some parallels after I became a member.

# OLYMPIC MOUNTAIN RESCUE

||||||||||||||||||||||||||||||||||||||||||||||||||||||||||||||||||||||||||||||||||||||||||||||||||||||||||||||

WHILE SERVING IN the U.S. Army Military Police, I was about to turn twenty-one and thought I'd like to try a different job in the Army and make it a career of it. I wanted to be an airborne ranger and decided to look into jump school. I talked to our Top or First Sergeant about it. He discouraged me and said I was too small, because one of the requirements would be to drag a 150-pound man out of harm's way. I bought that and decided I should stop thinking about an Army career. When I left I had an honorable discharge after completing my contract. I'd liked the structure, but my options were too limited there.

Two years later, I passed all the physical tests for the California Highway Patrol. I'd met all the requirements for their police academy including dragging a 150-pound dummy to safety. At the time, I was overjoyed at the prospect of becoming a highway patrol woman. A couple of days later, I remembered Top telling me that I couldn't budge 150 pounds and became furious. A fat old man had ruined my hopes of a career in the service for no reason. I later learned that there were no women in the U.S. Army airborne rangers in 1981, and the first women who graduated from that school were army officers in 2015.

When I married my first husband shortly after being invited to the police academy, my hopes for the CHP were dashed, because he said, "No way is my wife getting shot at." I was 27 years old and by then I'd lost count of how many times men had told me what I could and couldn't do.

Olympic Mountain Rescue is a volunteer organization in the state of Washington. I thought that since I'd served in a combat support unit in the U.S. Army, the discipline I gained would make me an asset to any mountain rescue unit. In the service I'd been taught the importance of being able to do your part without question, especially when it came to matters of life and death.

After I submitted a climbing resumé, I was interviewed, and admitted as a volunteer. I'd have to wait a while before I was allowed to go on a mission, because it would take months to learn all the essential rescue techniques. What that boiled down to was attending mandatory training sessions for about a year. I had no problem with that, but didn't like the long drive to the headquarters in Bremerton, Washington.

At my first meeting, there were only two other women there besides Jan, and about a dozen men. Most of the members were older than me, and I was no youngster in my early forties. During the time I was there, only one other woman joined.

She was in her late twenties and a top-notch climber, but left in less than a year. She'd decided that the macho atmosphere was unfair, and told me she rarely got paged. She complained that men in the unit treated her as an inferior without cause. I understood what she meant but tried to talk her into staying. She wouldn't waste her time placating men who treated her as a subordinate, and left.

I was very excited when I got my first page from Mountain Rescue. I was called and told we'd begin a mission early in the morning down on the Queets River. I had to get up in the middle of the night to get to the Queets by daybreak. OMR needed to call everyone available because they needed a big search party.

We got to the river at about seven in the morning, as the sun was rising. An 82-year-old man had gone fishing with his son and grandson on Saturday and disappeared. If he was still alive, he would've been exposed to the elements for almost two days. A helicopter was on the way to assist in the search.

That area along the Queets River is a lush rainforest. The woods we entered were an enchanted emerald green world full of majestic pine trees, ferns, fungi of every shape and color. The river was a wild, rain-swollen torrent. I watched the incredible turbulence of the swift current as we crossed in the inflatable boat, and could feel the powerful river pummeling us. The shore was covered with large, smooth river rocks and I saw many with a vein of white quartz running through them. The downed trees in the log jam were massive. They must have lived over a hundred years and then come crashing down into the river. The mist was gently lifting, and the rising sun spread fingers of light through the dark forest.

As part of a team of four, we spent eight hours covering one quadrant on the map. It was exciting at first, but that excitement quickly wore off. To a casual observer we roamed the area aimlessly as if we were dementia patients looking for someone who wasn't there. The park rangers and other members of OMR were doing the same thing nearby. Our big prize that day was the discovery of a canteen the lost man had left behind. Shortly after that, our hearts sank when we found his footprints that led down to the river's edge.

The chopper buzzed overhead around four in the afternoon, and it flew back over us about an hour later. The dog handlers were ending their search for the day, and I was getting my tent out to set it up for the night, when we got the call on our walkie talkie that the man had been found! I wanted to meet the idiots who let their grandfather become hopelessly lost in the rainforest.

When I first saw the lost man, he reminded me of my Grandpa Jim. I wouldn't let my grandpa loose in woods like that, unless I was hoping he'd never come back. I asked him if he'd walked down to the river and he said, yes he had. I don't know if his family ever found out how close he came to going into that river and drowning, but he explained to me that he'd considered using his backpack to help him float. Damn good thing he didn't, because he would've been swallowed up, dragged down, beaten to a pulp on the rocks, and spit out somewhere downriver dead as a doornail.

I got a little closer to him and said, "I'm so glad to see you. Can I give you a hug?" He nodded, and I squeezed him and brushed my cheek against the stubble on his face. I was relieved he was okay.

Later, the park rangers bought a nice dinner for all the rescue personnel at the Kalaloch Lodge. During the meal I was surrounded by men from our unit who were jovial amongst themselves and swapped stories. I tried to talk to the men on either side of me and they both responded in a language of dull grunts that mostly consisted of "Huh" and "Nuh." I did get a couple of "Uh huhs" from the friendly one. I got home Tuesday at about one in the morning and lost some income from my job, but was satisfied knowing I'd helped save that sweet old man's life. The thought crossed my mind that I should've adopted him and brought him home.

George Mallory is my hero. He was the first man to attempt the tallest mountain in the world and died in the process in 1924. His body was found near the Hillary Step on Mt. Everest right about the same time I got my first invitation to climb Mt. Rainier.

Mountain Rescue hosted a dinner in Bremerton, and had a guest speaker, who talked about an expedition that recovered Mallory's body. I listened to the lecture and looked at a few objects Mallory had hauled up Everest. Then I picked up an old oxygen tank that weighed 8 pounds, and he carried four of those up there! I couldn't imagine how heavy his pack must have been. Mallory is my all-time favorite climber. There's a lot of things to love and admire about George. But when I discovered he liked to get naked in the mountains, I thought, "Wow" and really wished I'd known him. He was amazing!

The ice climbing class with mountain rescue was going to be held soon. It was the only other skill I needed in my bag of tricks to climb virtually any mountain. Up to that point I was good on snow and rock, but hoped to climb frozen waterfalls. I was chomping at the bit because I was so excited to learn about it.

On the hike up the Nisqually Glacier, with Mick, Joey, and Lionel, I got Joey to take a couple pictures of me. Because my face was comical with my nose basted in zinc oxide, I turned that into another Christmas postcard with clothes on. As we headed up, I was wearing my plastic climbing boots, which are perfect for ice climbing. We hiked up the moraine and then roped up to travel on the glacier.

It was the hottest time of the year, so the ice was melting like mad. We jumped a lot of crevasses, and the snow was dirty from rockfall. At about seven thousand, five hundred feet, Lionel picked out a camp spot and we set up tents. After that, we did some training for a few hours and then had dinner and got into our tents around eight o'clock. It would be light out for a couple more hours and I was snug as a bug and just inches away was Lionel. We said good night and that was that, no chit chat. I usually get irritated when people snore, but Lionel had this low grumbly noise that made me think I was next to a big teddy bear, and I slept just fine.

The next day, we all practiced ice climbing. When it was my turn, Mick lent me his top-of-the-line ice axes, and I gave them a five star rating, because they were really super light and made it very doable. After that, we packed up and headed back down. The descent on the moraine was no fun at all with rock debris and more crevasses than on the way up.

At last I was paying attention to getting pictures on my climbs and remembered to bring my camera again. I have more pictures from that climb than any other. One of my favorite things about that training event was the restaurant Lionel took us to on the way home. It's not far from the national park. I wish I could remember the name of that place. It's a small building, with frosty milkshakes and big juicy hamburgers and it was seriously good chow.

Homeward bound, I thought about my job. I had enough clients to pay the bills, but I was only living from month to month. I could put another personal trainer on my payroll, but I didn't want to do all that paperwork. I liked being the sole proprietor and did simple record keeping. I wanted to come up with a new income stream, but couldn't picture what that might be.

About a week after I returned from ice climbing, I was down at the pub having lunch. I pulled up a barstool and talked to my favorite bartender, Sylvia. She was a little older than me and we always had a lively conversation. I'd ordered the Caesar salad with chicken and a cold brew.

I sipped a Port Townsend IPA, and Sylvia said she'd met Bob Dylan at a party when she lived in L.A. I'd been hunched over the bar eating my salad, and I sat bolt upright, and my eyes widened in surprise "You've got to be kidding. He's one of my all-time favorite musicians." My mom had been a huge fan, too, and I came to love Bob at age four, because the bedtime lullabies that drifted into my bedroom were from his album *The Freewheelin' Bob Dylan* on my parent's turntable.

Sylvia gave me a sad smile and said, "He is a great artist, but it wasn't easy to talk to him." I pictured him surrounded by throngs of people and thought it must've been hard to get anywhere near him. Sylvia immediately burst my bubble. "I was with friends at a wild party, and they pointed him out to me sitting by himself at the side of the room."

"Really!"

"Yeah, he looked pretty down, and I went over and sat down next to him."

"What did he talk about?"

"Well, that was the problem. He didn't talk, and after I tried to get him to talk I ended up going back to hang out with my friends."

"You must be kidding! I would've asked him if he wanted to go do something else." Sylvia was shaking her head. "You don't understand. I did, but he didn't even answer me."

"Wow! That's really surprising." It wasn't surprising that Bob might not be the life of the party, but I would never have dreamed that he'd be alone at a social event. Sylvia got busy with other customers, and I finished my lunch, and left the pub with the lonely tune *"Don't think twice, it's alright"* echoing in my thoughts.

Like Bob, I'd had to say goodbye, honey babe a few times in my life, but I was lucky to have Clint in my life and hoped I'd never say goodbye to him.

# SO LONG, FAREWELL, I BID THEM ALL ADIEU

||||||||||||||||||||||||||||||||||||||||||||||||||||||||||||||||||||||||||||||||||||||||||||||||

I RAN DOWN Madison Avenue with a few bucks in my wrist wallet, to grab a latte at the end of my 3 mile run. Walking it off gave me time to examine brick buildings downtown with thoughts of buildering (free climbing buildings). En route to my favorite cafe I enjoyed all the simple things I usually didn't notice. The single, tall, nonfat latte tasted especially good that day.

Once home, showered and wrapped in a towel it was time for a fresh pot of French press coffee. Then I sat down at the computer. The sun streamed through my sliding glass doors and for a few minutes that was the best possible place to be, but that quickly changed.

Checking email, there was one from Uncle Barney, my biological dad's brother. He wrote that my bio dad had cancer and was in a hospice in Colorado. I sat and stared at the phone for a long time. My dad had vanished from my life when I was 2 years old, and I didn't owe him a damn thing — not even a phone call.

I looked like his twin sister, and I'd grown up wondering why he'd never even bothered to call me. So this call was awfully hard to make. With much practice beforehand, I managed to say, "Hi Dad." After that call, I gave him something he'd never given me, an idea of who I was. I assembled a photo album that included pictures of me and my kids over the years. I sat on the floor with the album in my lap, closed my eyes and thought about some of the times I wished I could've seen him, or just talked to him. Big fat tears rolled down my cheeks and I wrote, "I missed you all my life" on the last page.

Steve, my half-brother, called after my dad died and told me that he had loved the album. Steve was gay and had AIDS, and during his remaining years we became close. He kept that album and in a way it did double duty because Steve treasured it.

Clint was very sympathetic and comforting after I told him about my bio dad. He suggested we go up to Canada for a change of scene to celebrate Thanksgiving. That sounded good. I'd kill two birds with one stone, because it would help me clear my head and also spend quality time with my boyfriend.

To celebrate Thanksgiving, Clint and I took his truck and two kayaks to Tofino, British Columbia. At that point in our relationship, I think we were both wild about each other. We stayed at a resort on the beach, explored the area, checked out art galleries, and kayaked. We had drinks at the Wickaninnish Inn, had fun mispronouncing that name on purpose, and had dinner in nice restaurants. We talked about a few other places we might visit but I didn't need to go someplace special because I'd have been happy to be anywhere with him.

Spending time with Clint kept me busy, maybe too busy, and I wasn't climbing as much as I wanted to. The days were getting shorter as winter approached. I ran more often, practiced yoga, and found a new client.

I called my two younger boys and asked when they wanted me to take them shopping for school clothes. It was something I did with them each fall. Max couldn't wait to go, but Willy politely declined. Max and I made a date. He and I went out frequently on lunch dates for years. We had fun until about a year before he graduated from high school. I guess I became uncool at that point.

I was heartbroken when Maxwell was diagnosed with Cerebral Palsy at age two. Somehow he took it in stride and was a tough kid. In kindergarten a little girl sat down beside him in the lunchroom. His walker was next to the table, and she asked what was wrong with him. He responded, "Nothing's wrong with me, what's wrong with you?" I knew he was going to be just fine, because the kid had spunk.

I was outside every day for no less than forty-five minutes. That was my formula for surviving the dark months, because winter is tough, with either mist, rain, fog or clouds most of the time, but I never had a problem with the weather or lack of light because I self-medicated with an active lifestyle.

On Christmas Eve, Clint and I celebrated our holiday together. The gift he got from me was a teal pullover, and every time I saw him that winter he was wearing it, and I don't think he ever took it off. He spoiled me rotten, and gave me Harley leathers, then produced a bottle of Taittinger champagne. He pulled me into his arms, kissed me and told me to reach into his pocket. I felt beads and pulled out a pearl necklace with a gold clasp that I'd told him I'd longed for, and I thought he was too good to be true. My sons had a blast on the boat the next day, and that was the most perfect Christmas I'd ever had.

Mountain rescue snow training was on my calendar, and it was right up there with the ice climbing class. OMR held its annual snow training class at Hurricane Ridge that winter. There was a deep snowpack up there that year. The whole unit showed up, and we spent quite a bit of time assessing slope angles and their potential for avalanche.

All the Olympic National Park visitors had to leave before it got dark, but we were special and allowed to stay past sundown. A group of us decided to climb Mt. Angeles. We had a few guys who wanted to ski the avalanche chute and carried their skis up with them. The chute is a precipitous drop over a thousand feet down to the road. We climbed as a group over the steep hills on the way to the mountain, and it took a little longer than we'd bargained for. Route finding was okay, but we had to stop and check our position more than once because the accumulation of snow had disguised the appearance of the terrain.

We were climbing very near the top of that peak when Chad, one of our more colorful members, started singing the theme song to the Beverly Hillbillies. It wasn't easy making it over the rocks, but I found myself laughing as I gained the summit and was listening to his silly song.

At the top of Mt. Angeles, someone took a group photo. I've kept that one, and it's faded with age, but one of my favorites. We had a phenomenal, clear view there that winter, with the mountains blanketed in snow as far as the eye could see. It was a perfectly clear evening, and the interior of the Olympic Range, as well as the water in the Straits of Juan de Fuca, the San Juan Islands, and parts of Canada spread out below us.

The only time I fell on a mountain and feared for my life was on that icy descent from Mt. Angeles. I slipped, fell, and yelled "Falling," because I slid uncontrollably down that snow slope. I glanced down and saw that the steep angle of the slope was striped with patterns from chunks of snow that had skittered down until they disappeared off a cliff. If I hadn't clawed repeatedly on that ice-encrusted snow and anchored my axe, I wouldn't have been able to stop and could've had the same fate.

Thankfully, after I arrested my fall I hadn't pissed my pants, and a couple of big men in the unit said in gruff voices, "Good arrest." There was no pause, no concern whatsoever, but then again, I was a member of Olympic Mountain Rescue. I didn't need coddling, because what we did entailed some bumps and bruises and I didn't have a scratch on me. I was shaken by that fall, but reminded myself that I'd signed up for this.

There were any number of other pleasant activities I could've indulged in — a massage or a nice pedicure come to mind — but instead I chose to claw for dear life in an avalanche chute and began to question my sanity as we descended.

As we hiked back to the vehicles, I trudged slowly up a hill and carried a heavy load, because one of our members had gotten sick along the way, and I took some of her gear. I struggled up the hill with an aching back, and someone shouted, "Paula!" I turned toward the voice and saw the sun sinking behind Mt. Angeles. The water in the straits turned a faded dusty blue, and a brilliant robin's egg blue sky was painted with yellow, pink and orange. Mt. Angeles completely lit up and turned gold as the evening dusk settled behind it. I paused and then saw the rising moon and stars as they began to pop into the sky.

Finley snapped pictures of the mountain, and the intensity of light on Mt. Angeles turned him into a shining silhouette with a golden halo. I wished I'd had my camera for the umpteenth time to take that picture of him. He seemed to be an angel who had just flown down to join us from his home on the mountain of angels.

Olympic Mountain Rescue volunteers are unpaid, as though saving people's lives in dangerous conditions is valueless. So I shouldn't have been surprised to learn that they're not compensated for pulling standby duty at Hurricane Ridge either. Very few members of OMR volunteered to do that duty with any frequency, and I realized it wasn't a popular thing to do, but I loved it. Exploring the park when it was covered with a deep snow and had few people in it was terrific. My biggest problem was that no one wanted to leave the lodge, and it was like pulling teeth trying to find someone who would come play with me in the snow.

A couple months after climbing Mt. Angeles, I carpooled with a member of Mountain Rescue. We'd be meeting up with Chad for a weekend of standby duty at the Hurricane Hill Lodge. The woman who drove me up there gave me some pointers on Chad and cautioned me not to encourage him with more than a working interest. After I got to know Chad better, I wondered who she was trying to protect — him or me.

Chad was up there when I arrived, and I asked him if he'd consider going up Steeple Rock with me. He said sure. That surprised me, because no one in mountain rescue had ever left the lodge and joined me in the deep snow up there before. Chad wasn't much to look at; standing at about 5' 8" he was small and thin as a rail, but he'd been in OMR quite a bit longer than me and had a lot more experience climbing.

He got the radio before we took off, so we could call in if we ran into any problems. The hike up the logging road was an easy two miles. The snow was hard and sometimes icy. Everything looked different up there in the winter months, so I hardly recognized where we should leave the road. Steeple Rock is so steep that most of the snow just sluffs off it. More than 100 inches of snow had fallen that winter, and was piled up all around it. We kick-stepped up the hillside and then put on crampons because it was so icy.

The closer we got to the rock spire, I could see what looked like a good route to take. I had the route book in my hand and pointed to the description of a tree that helped mark the beginning of it. I said, "Hey, Chad, look there's the tree." He didn't look at my book, and I guess he must've believed I knew what I was talking about.

We got right to the base of a big crack by the tree and took off our crampons. Chad set our radio down and didn't pick it back up. He said he was sure we wouldn't need it. I didn't say anything and knew that the radio was a heavy chunk of metal, but of course, if we had any trouble, leaving the radio would be about the stupidest thing to do.

At the outset of that climb, I'd been glad that Chad joined me. Steeple Rock is a 200-foot pillar of stone, and I didn't want to climb it alone, especially in the winter. Chad led up a wide crack in the rock, and it became increasingly more difficult to find the next move. On the way up, my hands felt stiff and cold, and our boots seemed more harm than help, as were attempting to free solo on Steeple Rock in bitter, icy conditions.

We got to a point where we had no idea what to do next, and both knew we were in deep trouble. Chad said it would've been nice if *we'd* brought the radio. Without that radio we couldn't get any help and we sure wouldn't be missed for hours if it turned out that we needed it.

We'd come to a spot where the big crack ran out, and Chad said he'd take a look around the corner. We were stuck, dark clouds pressed in and I hoped it wouldn't snow. Alone and scared, with no possible way to down climb, there was only one thing to do. I had to find a way up. I didn't have options and needed to figure something out quick.

Since Chad had disappeared around the side of the peak, I'd lost track of time and wondered what the hell he was doing. I called his name and didn't get a response. I remembered when I fell on Mt. Angeles, and thought I was about to die, but I'd recovered from that fall because I never gave up and kept trying over and over to drive my axe into the snow. Giving up wasn't an option, so I reassessed the immediate area.

I thought of trying to mantle a rocky shelf next to me to see what was up there. That shelf jutted out and I couldn't use my feet to help me get up it. Mantling wasn't something I did well, and I'd have to place my palms at chest level, lean into the rock shelf, straighten my arms and try to lift my entire body weight with my triceps. Then I looked back at the icy rocks below, I envisioned falling to a cold death and got a rush. That must've fueled me, because I faced that rock outcropping and mantled right up onto that shelf.

Chad was still somewhere on the other side of Steeple Rock. When I stood up, looked around, and spotted a sling, my reaction was Hallelujah and Thank you Jesus! That's one sure way you know you are on a climbing route intended for a rope. I yelled, "Hey Chad, I found a sling!" He responded to me that time.

"I'm coming."

It didn't take him long to get back to where I was, and his eyes lit up when he saw the yellow, weather-beaten sling. "Great! I'll be on it in a sec." He rushed by and nearly knocked me off the rock shelf, on his way to the sling. I was cold, exhausted and pretty fed up with him right about then. He just took the lead again, as if I didn't exist. It didn't take rocket science to figure out what to do from there. We just went up to the split in the rock and crossed over to the other side. Once we got there, deep footprints showed us the rest of the way down.

When I was trapped on that ledge, I'd imagined the grim reaper at the base below me, and in the wind I thought I heard him whisper, "Down climb, Paula," but it wasn't my time to go.

After flogging ourselves on the wrong route with a myriad of possible unhappy endings, we'd both learned a very difficult lesson about how to climb Steeple Rock in the winter. Chad had nonchalantly leaned over and scooped up the radio off the snowy rocks where he'd dumped it and we quickly returned to the warm lodge. I looked up the wrong route we took in my mountain guide and that's when I learned it's rated 5.7. That climb had been a crap shoot, and the cost could've been losing fingers and toes, or worse. I especially dreaded losing my toes, and was relieved that all ten were intact, because there are few things I enjoy more than a good pedicure.

At Hurricane Hill on standby duty about a month later, I decided to do a reconnaissance mission and check out a shelter. I told Kyle I'd be looking for "Waterhole" and then come back. I took a radio with me because I'd never been there before. Armed with my custom correct map that had Waterhole clearly indicated on it, I was prepared.

People in OMR talked about that place, and I wanted to know exactly how to get there. Once I knew where it was, I'd camp in the shelter if I wanted to someday. The place is a tiny cabin with a small wood stove in it, and I was told it had room for six inside. The average person might not want to stay overnight, but it would be another card in my deck for outdoor adventures.

A park ranger named Will Jones gave me a lift. That was his last year with the park service. He was about 25 years older than me and ready to retire. I thanked him and realized I didn't need my snowshoes; the snow was compact and I did a four-mile hike in about an hour and a half.

I only saw one person before I got to Waterhole — a man jogging in snowshoes. Once I saw the radio repeater tower, I knew I was almost there. The closer I got, I could smell smoke, and then I saw the little cabin, with smoke that curled up out of a stove pipe in the roof.

A ladder led to the door. I knocked, and someone said, "Come in." I held the door open and waited for my eyes to adjust, and then I saw the park's resident hermit, Stan. I'd met him once before when I was doing OMR volunteer work at the lodge. He was a mysterious character who seemed to be able to survive in the wilderness with no permanent shelter.

That day we talked for about 45 minutes, and I didn't learn much about him, because I did most of the talking. As a hermit, his conversational skills were rusty, but he did tell me that he didn't have a job or a home. My hair was dyed a deep copper red, and he said, "When you opened the door all I could see was your silhouette, and the light shining on your red hair made it a flaming halo. I wondered if you were an angel or a devil." I laughed and asked him what he thought now. He told me deadpan that he wasn't sure.

Stan was 15–20 years older than me, and a recluse who subsisted on next to nothing. I'd also heard some gossip that he was a Vietnam vet who was fed up with society in general. Rumor had it that his disgust with humankind was why he chose to live alone in the wilderness. Stan was a unique character. I momentarily considered giving him my contact information, because he must've known the best routes to a couple of rock features I was interested in exploring. I decided against that and couldn't imagine how I could hike with someone who not only didn't have a phone, but more importantly didn't even have an address. If he hired a matchmaker, they'd have a tough time reaching him to send him on a date.

That night on a padded bench in my sleeping bag I made some plans for the next day. The last time Chad was here, we'd gotten into a jam on Steeple Rock. After all the time that had gone into finding the correct winter route, I'd have to use it. I asked the other two OMR members if they wanted to join me, but they passed. The hike in was much better this time. Not only did I not need crampons, but I actually knew where I was going. With no ice at the base of the rock it looked as if climbing with ice axe, boots, and my helmet would do. Crampons were in my backpack just in case it was icy up there, and the radio was definitely a must.

A solo attempt on Steeple Rock would prove to me that I could make it up there any time of the year by myself, and I was confident I could do it alone that winter. I had no trouble and found the ascent began in someone else's bootprints. About halfway up, the path was unclear and my first thought was to reconnoiter the snowy slope, but I didn't have to do that and got back onto the right route. At last I reached the summit!

Wow! That had taken me three tries to figure out. I wasn't cold, scared, or angry and that might've been a first for me. I still didn't have a cell phone, so I used my little camera and took a picture of my ice axe on the summit. Even with all the snow, the beautiful shades of red and gold colored lichen on the rocks appeared clearly in my photo.

The mist was heavy and though I wanted to take a picture of the lodge below, the clouds obscured it. I'm the only one who can appreciate that photo. It's a picture of a rock with an ice axe next to it but it's one of my favorite photos.

I grabbed my radio and made a call to Jan in the lodge:

"OMR 1, this is OMR 2."

"This is OMR 1, go ahead."

"Well, Jan, I've looked high and I've looked low, but there are no single men up here!"

"Maybe I should send Will up there."

"It's beautiful here, but some testosterone sure would be nice. OMR 2 out."

Olympic Mountain Rescue is an essential organization whose members have saved people's lives. In OMR I snapped at the carrot on the end of the mountain rescue stick for over two years, until my jaws ached from the effort and then I quit. I think they didn't know or care about my ability to perform under pressure. I learned some skills in that unit, but my experience in OMR was in effect more like banging my head on a rock wall for the fun of it.

Like the Army they never found out what I had to offer, and to this day I have no idea why I was inducted. I thought I'd played by their rules, but don't think I got the right rule book. I kept hoping that OMR would wake up, smell the coffee and give this little gal a chance to do what she signed up for. But sadly, they never did.

# WALKING IN THE MOUNTAINS

IIIIIIIIIIIIIIIIIIIIIIIIIIIIIIIIIIIIIIIIIIIIIIIIIIIIIIIIIIIIIIIIIIIIIIIIIIIIIIIIIIIIIIIIIIIIIIIIIIIIIIIIIIIIIIIIIIIIIIIIIIIIIIIIIIIIIIII

AFTER RESIGNING FROM mountain rescue, I took a close look at my finances. A percentage of the income I earned went to the local gym, and since I was an independent contractor, it was a fair deal. That actually worked fine for years, until they decided to bring personal trainers on to their staff. I realized that my days were numbered as freelance trainer in that club, because new members were encouraged to hire a staff trainer. That would soon cramp my lifestyle. I even mentioned to the gym owner that my work was slowing down, and I only had ten appointments that week.

He said, "Isn't that good?"

I told him, "No. Good is about twenty appointments a week." I couldn't work for him because the wages he paid were too low. I hadn't tried to find a job in Seattle, but decided I needed to look into that.

That spring I got a job at the Seattle Athletic Club working as a personal trainer and continued to work with a few clients on the island. I found that I wasn't coming out ahead, because the health club in Seattle only paid me half of what I charged on the island for training appointments. I didn't have enough clients to make it feasible to continue working there.

My efforts to make more money in the big city failed and climbing had really taken a back seat during that time. I was pleased that after my job in Seattle flopped, I was rewarded with a grand tour on Clint's big Harley. He took me on a motorcycle ride late one afternoon and invited me to ride out to Sturgis with him. I said, "Wow, I'd love that!" I'd only heard about the biggest motorcycle rally in the world, and knew it would have to be an amazing event. He said we'd leave in two weeks. Since my workload was light it was easy for me to reschedule my clients. After that, I couldn't wait for the road trip to begin.

On the trip to Sturgis, Clint drove his big red Harley, and we went up into Canada and back down into Montana just for fun. We camped a lot, and the closer we got to Sturgis, the more motorcycles we saw on the road. We'd been chilled to the bone in Canada and roasted as we drove south into South Dakota. Clint was so clever and had drilled holes in the bottom of one of the metal saddle bags, filled it with ice, and packed it with beer. When we stopped for a rest we'd have a cold beer. That made the hot part of the ride so much better.

Devils Tower was on the way, and just before we got there the road turned into a sea of bikes. The continuous roar of motorcycle engines filled the atmosphere from then on. We passed through Deadwood and drove into Sturgis. Every parking space was filled, with bikes parked two rows deep on the median. We managed to squeeze in and park. Clint wanted to talk to a tattoo artist before we went to the Buffalo Chip Campground. I waited outside, and a man walked up and asked me if he could take my picture. I said sure. He just stood there looking at me and didn't even have a camera. Then he walked away, and I was confused. Clint told me that's what men say when they want women to flash them, and I laughed.

We got to the campground just in time to experience a horrendous thunderstorm that swept in so quickly we barely knew what hit us. One moment it was sunny and warm and then pouring rain with powerful wind. It was over almost as quickly as it started. I couldn't believe it, and was relieved it was over. I managed to get clean in a clawfoot bathtub that had no walls and was open for public viewing. I had a bit of an audience, but I got clean.

We ate at one of the food stalls near the stage, and had beer in a bar that sprayed a fine mist overhead refreshing us in the summer heat. I was tired and grumpy because I hadn't slept well. Our tent was pitched very close to both the stage and a dirt road with non-stop motorcycles roaring by. Clint wanted to watch the Blues Travelers perform, and I told him to enjoy himself, but that I needed to rest. The loud music was impossible to muffle even with my earplugs, so I didn't rest.

The following day I was in a foul mood, but we stuck it out for another day, then Clint suggested we go home. We'd both looked forward to Sturgis, but I wasn't having a good time. The sky was black and threatened to rain again and he said we'd had some fun and that's all he'd wanted to do. What a relief it was to hear that.

After all, staying in a campground that became a mud slurry with each passing thunderstorm and wrestling my tent to the ground in high winds was not on my list of things to do. Attempting to sleep with a loud rock band a stone's throw away was a killjoy and a skill I didn't want to acquire. Top that off with the constant roar of Harley engines 24/7 right outside my tent, and I was in a continuous state of agitation. Sturgis was exciting and very memorable, but its effect on me was that I became an exhausted, complaining ballbuster. Clint aptly referred to the trip as "The Good, Bad and the Ugly."

After we got back from the Sturgis road trip, it took me a day or two to recover from its toll on me and I gave a lot of thought to our relationship. I'd talked to Kathy, my step-mother about it, and she warned me not to push him for marriage. I thought we'd been a couple long enough and decided it was time to make a serious commitment, so I cut to the chase and asked him to marry me. His piercing blue eyes searched mine as he told me he couldn't do it. I loved him, but told him it was over between us. He got angry and shouted some choice words at me.

I wanted a committed relationship, and for me that meant marriage. If I'd continued to date him, that might prevent me from meeting the man I would marry. Ending it with Clint hurt like hell, but I was trying to be logical for a change and use my head instead of only listening to my heart.

Focusing on work was a good thing after that break-up, I had to re-build my clientele and it helped to distract me from my feelings. I really had to scramble and figure out how to increase my income ASAP because my rent would be due in a couple of weeks and my bank account was not in good shape. Breaking up with Clint had cut over $600.00 a month from my income, so I brainstormed trying to think of something.

I got a call from a girlfriend who'd moved to Seattle. I hadn't seen her for a few years, so I was delighted to hear from her. We talked about this and that and then she told me she was thinking of starting a service as a dominatrix and wondered if I'd like to join her. She was one of my favorite people with an offbeat sense of humor and imaginative, avant garde ideas. Talking with her was always a treat, so I had her explain how she planned to do that, and then told her it sounded like a good business plan, but no thanks. When I hung up I thought, what amazing timing. I'd wanted to make more money, just not that way.

When I'm under pressure, I often come up with a pretty good plan. I decided to invest in six pairs of Redfeather snowshoes to take people into the mountains. I could earn nearly $250 per trip while I guided a group and provided the snowshoes. That would help cover my living expenses, because in order to feed my climbing fever, I had to feed the climber. I'd already signed up clients for a hike in the mountains and needed to get people on the snowshoe outing.

My favorite cafe was in the Village Green, and I hoped they might let me display a poster for my snowshoe trip. Looking around while standing in line there I noticed Kris was right behind me waiting to order his coffee. He was tall, blond, and had nice features. I'd seen him in the gym now and then doing a kickass workout. I talked to him a couple of times and learned that he was — in addition to many other things — a climber. A magazine article about rock climbing in Thailand had recently caught my eye and I wanted to do that very badly, but didn't want to go alone. I said hi to Kris and brought up the idea of rock climbing in Thailand.

He said that my idea sounded great, but that his wife would kill him if he climbed with me. I thought about that for a while, but when I learned that his wife was a gorgeous model, it cast doubt on his assertion. I was no competition at all compared to that tall, photogenic, brunette and was the complete opposite of her. He'd told me that he jumped out of planes to ski, so I was confident that he didn't lack the courage to climb cliffs overhanging the ocean. I couldn't think of anyone else I knew who might be up for such a sporting vacation that included deep water climbing. It was a departure from what most people did on holiday, so I shelved that magazine in hopes of needing it for reference someday.

The owners of the cafe wouldn't let me post my material, so I went to the Streamliner. I sat at the counter and talked to the owner, Christina about the snowshoe trip. She put my flyer up right away in the window by the door. I had my favorite meal — the roast turkey sandwich with cranberry sauce and potato salad. Then Doug sat down next to me. He was an adorable gentle giant. Tall as a lumberjack, but so shy that by comparison I was an extrovert. I smiled and asked him what he'd been doing lately. He answered in his warm, deep voice with a slight stutter, that he was building a new home. We talked for a while and when his meal arrived, I slid off the barstool, gave him a peck on the cheek and noticed his beautiful blue eyes had widened a little. In response to my kiss, he clapped his hand to the spot my lipstick had marked and held it for a moment, as if trying to capture something.

At the door I paused to admire the huge monkey tail pine tree across the street. And what to my wondering eyes did appear, but Kevin getting out of a red Land Rover. He waved to me, so I crossed the street and he told me that he'd hoped to run into me. I'd met him at a party the year before, but he was married and didn't look twice at me. I hadn't talked to him much, but he was always friendly. I was surprised when he said he'd been looking for me. I barely knew him and wondered if he needed a personal trainer. I asked him what he'd been up to lately and how his wife Mindy was doing.

Kevin returned my greeting, but completely ignored my question and told me he wanted to hike up Mt. Shasta in Oregon and wondered if I knew an attractive single woman who might join him. I said I'd like to do that hike. He said that would be great, but did I know another single lady who might want to go too? Well, that told me he wasn't after me which was a relief. He explained that we'd fly down to Oregon in his plane and make it a day trip. I knew a woman who'd love that. I told him I had a lovely friend about my age, but that she was married. He said that would be okay.

I called up Lillith, and told her that she and I had been invited to fly down to Oregon and hike Mt. Shasta. I wanted to know if she could go. She was into hiking and beginning to get into climbing. She was delighted and accepted the invitation right away. I knew she was keen on airplanes and suspected she might get some flying instruction, but I didn't tell her that.

Kevin picked up Lillith and me in a late model, white, Lincoln Continental and took us to the airport in Bremerton. I loved that car because it was so luxurious. It felt like we were being chauffeur-driven in a limo on our way to the airport so we could go on a hike! That was the royal treatment, and I was a princess for the day in my shorts and T-shirt.

When we arrived at the small airport, we were ushered into a beautiful town car and drove into a campground where we began our hike. We couldn't have gone there on a more perfect day. As we hiked up everything around us was blue and white. The endless sky dominated, and the perfect mountain was capped with snow. Lillith and I kept going too fast, and if I'd been there without her I would've slowed down. She's a jackrabbit, but I enjoyed her company more than Kevin's and kept pace with her. He'd just have to keep up.

As we tramped in difficult loose scree on Cooper's Spur, the years of abuse on rocky trails and mountains took its toll on my tired Asolo boot, and one yawned widely in desperation, as the leather upper peeled open to flap in the rare, high mountain breeze setting my sweaty, sock covered toes free. My clever girlfriend took a couple of brightly colored hair scrunchies and deftly reaffixed the leather upper back onto the sole. We all had a good laugh about the new look I sported, but we didn't know how long Lil's debut surgical procedure would last. So we turned around and descended to the parking area. That hike had been a first-rate romp.

On the way home in the plane that evening, I saw how enthusiastically Kevin encouraged Lil to use the controls on the plane. I was surprised at her reluctance to play with the levers, knobs and dials. The dash on the plane was a fascinating sort of thing and the green glow of many lights invited someone to fiddle with it.

I considered how Kevin had treated us both like queens for a day and wondered what had inspired his gift of that magical trip. I wished that he'd had a note pinned to his chest that would've given me a clue. I learned later that the note would have been a prescription with an antidote for the pain and loneliness he experienced because his wife had left him.

Lillith would've been fun to rock climb with, but she was still mostly into hiking, not rock climbing. I decided to go to Peshastin Pinnacles by myself. The weather was fine, and there were bound to be other climbers there. That was my second time at Peshastin, and it was a kick! Between climbing at rock gyms, and my outdoor experience, I'd finally caught on to the friction technique of slab climbing. Wearing rock climbing shoes, I'd put the sole of my shoe flat on the gritty rock wall, and with the aid of a pebble or two for my fingers, I'd move up. I imagined that from afar friction climbers must look like flies on a wall there.

Danielle and I had made a plan to rock climb at Exit 38. I hadn't been up there for over a year, and couldn't imagine anything else I'd rather do, until I got a call from my youngest son Max. He invited me to his football jamboree on that same weekend. I usually invited Max to do things with me, and this was the first time he'd invited me to do something with him, so I was tickled pink and told him I'd definitely be there.

Born with Cerebral Palsy, Max couldn't walk without assistance until he was seven years old. His physical therapist encouraged him to use walking canes with arm support, but he was determined to learn to walk unaided, and has a lot of scars on his face as a result. It seems he's hardheaded in more ways than one, and I think he and I have a lot more in common than pretty blond hair.

I knew Max wanted my support when he asked me to come to his jamboree. He'd only be a kid for a few more years, so Exit 38 could wait. I canceled with Danielle and told her we'd do something again soon. I enjoyed watching Max at the football game, and was very proud of him and took pictures.

The flyers I'd posted about my hike didn't seem to work at all; the only people who were on the Mt. Townsend hike were all friends and clients. I'd noticed that all my flyers and posters routinely vanished from the bulletin boards within a day or two after I put them up around town. I wondered if I should run an ad in the newspaper. It must have been just a coincidence that the health club was trying to promote hikes and climbs around that time too.

I always seemed to find something wrong on climbs and that worried me, even though this was just a hike. I hoped I wouldn't be too anxious because I couldn't afford to lose potential customers. I couldn't wire my jaws shut because I was the leader in the group. I'd just have to cross my fingers and try to behave myself.

Mt. Townsend is a place I'd hiked and snowshoed a lot over the years, and I knew the trail like the back of my hand. My last hike there had been with Jacob, a member of mountain rescue. He'd been lagging on the way up, but looked like he was in great shape. I didn't understand why he was so slow, until we sat down to eat lunch at the summit and he produced a six pack of bottled beer!

On the Mt. Townsend hike, everyone carpooled from a large parking lot at a local supermarket. The hiking group consisted of myself, Shelly, Jim, Jim's son Austin, and Amelia. I was certain that if it went well, my clients would tell their friends and soon I'd have plenty of paying customers to lead into the mountains. We were really lucky that the weather cooperated. In November, there's usually a better chance of rain than not.

I'd talked to everyone except Austin about what they should bring and I knew his dad would've talked to him about that. Plus, those two had done a lot of camping and hiking. I'd taken Amelia up into the Valley of the Silent Men on an all-girl hike, but this was a whole new ballgame for Shelly.

Everyone on the hike was pleasant and enjoyed each other's company. They managed to stay together and kept an even pace. I was accustomed to reining in hikers who couldn't seem to stay with the group, or inspiring a dawdler. In my hiking experience I'd learned to be gentle and then firm with hikers who raced ahead of the group. I sympathized with them because of my problems with going slow on glaciers, but that was the extent of my compassion toward hikers. I was about to find out on Mt. Townsend if I had enough patience and compassion to be a good guide.

It's not difficult to go into the woods and become disoriented and lost. The older man who got lost near the Queets River was a good example of that. For that reason, we had to be able to see each other at all times. When someone needed a party separation, shorthand for taking a leak, that was the only time someone could be out of sight.

We came out of the woods and saw the most panoramic view of the Cascades from the Olympic Mountains. Naturally, everyone wanted to take pictures. I was amazed at how differently I felt about the slow pace and people taking pictures. It didn't bother me at all. I wondered if it was because I'd been there so many times before, or if it was because I was being paid to provide a pleasant outing. I was pretty sure it was actually because I was responsible for their well-being. I was relieved when I noticed that the urge to move on wasn't there. Then it occurred to me that this was what patience felt like! It's a quiet little thing and I didn't recognize it at first having had limited experience with it.

I knew once we got past the most scenic spot, the trail went up in steep switch backs to the top. I got right next to Shelly, because I wanted to be able to encourage her or take her pack if need be. She was a trooper and didn't need me at all. We rested, drank water and grabbed a quick snack a couple of times and after three hours of steady uphill hiking, we reached the top of Mt. Townsend.

Shelly was elated. She announced to everyone that this was the first time she'd climbed a mountain. I didn't want to burst her bubble, so I didn't tell her that since no technical climbing was involved, it was just a hike. I thought about the hike when I got home and realized

I'd experienced both patience and compassion on that hike and was flabbergasted. I'd thought I would chase them both to the ends of the earth and then they decided to join me and spend the whole day with me. In retrospect that run-in with patience was a godsend, and I can still access it from time to time.

One of the women on that hike, Amelia, asked me to accompany her on a visit to see her brother in Montana. She said she'd like me to help her with her workouts on the way there and amp up her cardiovascular training while we traveled. I'd gotten to know Amelia well and helped her to drop some pounds. She was working with me to help her reach her goal weight and was doing a good job. I wanted to help her stay on track with exercise. She would be paying me well, and I was able to take off for a three-day weekend, so I said yes.

I figured getting paid to do some driving was fine and I'd see some sights along the way. I didn't mind working with a traveling client, and the money was an extra perk. I thought maybe she'd take me with her on longer vacations if this worked out.

When we were driving home from Montana, Amelia mentioned that she had quite a bit of marijuana in the trunk of the car. She explained that part of the reason for visiting her brother was to get several months' worth of dope for her personal use. I've never used recreational drugs, but I don't care if other people do and figured that's their own choice. A couple of beers or the occasional martini works great for me, and it's legal. Pot hadn't been legalized at that time, but I didn't worry about it. If we got pulled over, the cop would see a couple of attractive women and we'd smile brilliantly and that would be the end of that.

Coming down from Snoqualmie Pass, I was driving and Amelia said we might miss the next ferry. I really wanted to get home and missing that ferry wasn't part of my plan. I stepped on it and noticed I was doing 80 miles per hour. There was a lot of traffic, and I was bobbing and weaving around other cars, when we heard a siren go off.

Amelia was smoking a joint in the car and sounded like she was about to choke to death when the siren started. Her window was down, and I put mine down as fast as I could. She extinguished the joint and I have no idea what she did with it. She started taking copious amounts of breath mints and simultaneously spraying something around in the car. I pulled over and a state trooper pulled in right behind me. He just sat there for a while, as Amelia and I freaked out. Then he sauntered around to my window and asked me for my license and registration. He wanted to know why I was driving so fast, and I told him truthfully that I didn't want to miss the ferry. He rested his forearm in my open window and leaned in toward the interior of the car. His head swiveled and he kept that position for a few minutes while he talked to Amelia. I don't remember what that cop said, but I do remember picturing us both in handcuffs. I was sure we were in deep trouble and felt like I might puke.

I knew he must have gotten a whiff of dope, because I thought I could still smell it. Orange clashed with our complexions, and I was sure we'd both look terrible in matching orange jumpsuits. This was quite a test for Amelia's aerosol spray. We sat there for a suspenseful 5 to 10 minutes and Amelia who is fair skinned looked even whiter if that's possible. But instead of yanking me out through the window by my shirt collar, the stater stood up and started writing a ticket.

Once we got back into traffic, we heaved sighs of relief and busted out laughing. I had a ticket for 125 dollars that Amelia offered to pay, but I wouldn't let her. After all, I was the driver who'd chosen to speed. That was the first and last time I accompanied a client on a trip. The scenario of the cop pulling us over had turned out almost as I'd imagined it, except when he walked up to the car we didn't smile.

Once I got home, I returned to the work week grind, and got people signed up for my group snowshoe trip. I had five people signed up for the "Winter Wonderland" guided trip at Hurricane Ridge. I showed my clients some of the best photos I'd taken there and they jumped at the opportunity to go. There was only one man on this snowshoe trip.

Robert was very visually oriented and an internationally renowned photographer. He also took great pride in his physique, and that's why I got to know him. The day we met, I was in line at Bainbridge Bakers where I often lingered, dressed in my usual jog bra and capri tights. While I studied the riddle of the day posted in front of the espresso machine, a man behind me said, "I want the male equivalent of your shoulders." I turned around and met Robert, who became a new client that day.

When I described this trip, Robert asked me how many calories snowshoeing burned. I told him it could be 600 per hour, depending on conditions. That sold him on the spot. Amelia and the others wanted to go when I described how beautiful it was. Only one of the women was concerned about her ability to do it, and I assured her she'd be fine.

At the entrance of the national park we were told at the gate there might be some icy patches on the road, and to pull over and put chains on if that happened. The ranger also said that we'd have to leave if it began to snow. The drive up was clear and dry. We all fit nicely in Robert's Toyota land cruiser, and the four women in the back chattered away incessantly. Suddenly most of the women in the back were laughing with delight, because they'd all been raised in Minnesota, and I got to listen to their thoughts on that as we got closer to the lodge.

We put on snowshoes because the snowy trail really was a winter wonderland. All the trees were heavily laden with snow, because there had recently been a big winter storm up there. It looked like no one had been on that trail in the past day or two, so it was hard work to break trail on snowshoes in deep powdery snow that came up to my knees. There was a heavy, low mist and the views were obscured, but the snowy landscape made up for the mountain views.

Trudging along with my hiking party in tow, I recalled the winter wonderland I'd known years before on the farm. The fields were solid white, and I'd make my way across them to the pond with ice skates slung over my shoulder. That pond was so close to the woods that it was mostly clear of snow. I'd swoop and carve as I slashed the ice with my blades. On the way back to our big old colonial style home, I'd make a couple snowballs in hopes of surprising one of my brothers. I stopped on the trail, made a snowball and turned to hit Amelia squarely in the middle of her chest. Before I knew it, we were all in the middle of a snowball fight!

We dusted ourselves off and Robert was right on my heels and raring to go, so I put him in the lead to break trail; that worked, and he got the calorie burn he wanted. We didn't get to Hurricane Hill, because I was keeping an eye on the weather, and the sky looked heavy and ready to drop a load of snow. I got the group turned around, and when we got to the lodge we posed for a group picture. I'd made a good call about when to turn around, because the clouds were beginning to lighten their load. It felt like the temperature was rapidly dropping as we got into the 4-wheel-drive-vehicle and tiny snowflakes decorated our parkas.

Since Robert was from Australia, I should've realized he probably had limited experience driving on ice. He careened around a hairpin turn and nearly lost it on the ice. The vehicle leaned hard, and my view out the passenger side window was a frightening descent hundreds of feet down the mountainside. My whole body tensed up, but he corrected just in time. All the women gave him hell and he slowed way down.

After the last two guided trips in the mountains, it was beginning to look like I might be able to start another business as a mountain guide. So far, I'd delivered just what I had promised, and everyone had a great time. I was glad that my lack of patience didn't seem to be an issue. It was possible that I could even take a few people on climbs as well, and that was a goal. I had to find a better way to advertise and research the insurance, because if I was paid to climb I'd be living the dream.

Something I really wanted to work on besides making more money was getting along with male climbing partners. I decided I should try to think of them as my mountain brothers. That had happened naturally with Eddy. So when Chad asked me to climb Mt. Rainier with him and Joey, I thought it would be the perfect time to try that 'mountain brother' idea.

Chad told me he'd lead the climb and wanted to know if I'd be able to go with them. I said yes, even though I didn't have a lot of confidence in Chad as a safe climbing partner. They were both strong, healthy men and younger than me, so I reasoned that this climb on Rainier could be the one I'd been waiting for. I imagined we'd climb to the summit at a better pace than I ever had before, and those two would probably be cracking jokes all the way to the top.

I did wonder why he'd invited me. He must've had other choices for climbing partners. I'd only been on the DC Route once before and didn't know the terrain very well, but I did have a decent reputation as an alpine climber and assumed that must have been why he'd invited me.

There'd only been one good thing about that last mountain rescue meeting I'd attended. A woman in the unit told me several mountain rescue members had planned a climb the year before. They'd intended to invite me, because they agreed that if I went they'd probably summit, but ended up having to cancel the trip. I was surprised, because prior to hearing that I'd been under the impression that everyone in the unit thought I was a pain in the ass.

That climb with Chad and Joey would be my third summit there and I went downstairs in the small kitchen department at Town and Country to get the big hug from my buddy Fred. When I told him I was going back up Mt. Rainier again, he was happy for me and squeezed me tightly. I stocked up on Cadbury Fruit and Nut candy bars and lemon drops then went home.

On the morning of the anticipated climb, I got up early, took a quick shower, ate my favorite breakfast and double-checked my pack. My La Sportiva boots and gaiters were already in the truck and I was feeling sad. I wished I could share my joy of climbing with at least one of my sons or a close friend. As I filled my coffee thermos the phone rang and Chad informed me that Joey was sick, so we'd go without him the next day.

I'd rescheduled more clients, and went on a nice long run to clear my head. As the day dragged on, I realized that my friend Tom hadn't returned any of my phone calls lately, so I decided to go on a reconnaissance mission, because he'd apparently fallen off the face of the planet. He'd recently moved back to the island after living in Arizona and I just couldn't spend enough time with him. I had missed him like crazy when he was living in the Southwest.

When he would disappear periodically, and I was pretty sure he was on the island, I'd have to scout him out. There was only one other place I knew that I might find him besides his boat or the diner, and that was the bar at Isla Bonita. My kids and I ate at that restaurant and enjoyed it there, but I didn't like going into the bar. Unfortunately, Tom did. The bar was a dark, smoky den of drunks, and I avoided it like the plague. The drinks were cheap and he could hang out there for hours drinking, smoking, and shooting the breeze. I decided to bite the bullet and go there.

I walked in and immediately got a couple of low wolf whistles as I slowly made my way down the length of the bar until, and lo and behold I found him. He was talking to a Leonardo Di Caprio look alike named Julian. I tapped Tom on the shoulder and launched into the Spanish Inquisition.

"Where have you been? Why haven't you called me? What's going on?" Julian spun around, hopped onto an empty barstool next to him and patted the one he'd just been sitting on, all the while he was giving me a lascivious grin as he stared at my boobs.

Tall Tom slowly turned toward me, smiling, with a glass of something on the rocks that tinkled as he swirled it. "Paula! It's good to see you too." How I loved the sound of his voice. It was a woozy version of Cary Grant's.

"Sorry Tom, I was worried about you."

"Don't worry about me. I'm fine. Hungry?"

"No, I just ate. Well, I'm glad you're fine, but you need to get back to me once in a while. Can we get together and go out on your sailboat soon?"

"Next week?"

"Okay. Promise to call?" I was really uncomfortable and wanted to get out of there fast.

"You know I will."

I didn't know that, but remembered to tell him, "I'm climbing Mt. Rainier tomorrow."

"Again! You're a crazy woman." He smiled and raised his glass a little, as if to toast me.

Julian, who'd long since turned his back to me, glanced over his shoulder and said dismissively in Russian, "*ty sumasshedshaya suka.*" I had no idea what that meant, but his tone and body language told me it wasn't good.

I smiled and gave Tom a peck on the cheek. He's well over six feet tall and it was a stretch to meet my mark even though he was seated on a barstool. I nearly ran out of there because the combination of Julian and the wolf whistles had made me feel like steak on the hoof surrounded by hungry wolves. I went across the street, got a rosemary chicken at T&C, and went home.

Chad called me early in the morning and told me Joey was better and would go with us after all. That news worried me, but I'd already committed to being in the climbing party. We carpooled from the Central

Market in Poulsbo. Chad must've had his reasons when he picked our departure date, but he hadn't shared them with me. Four climbers had died on Mt. Rainier in the past month and Joey had just come off a high fever and either one of those things was a good reason to do it later that year.

At Rainier National Park, we got the permit to climb, but the rangers were concerned about the weather. We were there on a bright sunny day, but were told a storm was predicted in the near future. The rangers warned us that if we saw any signs of bad weather approaching, we'd have to descend and not try to tough it out or we might get fried in a lightning storm. I appreciated that they shared that with us, but boastful Chad informed them that he and Joey were both members of Olympic Mountain Rescue, as if that had some bearing on the weather. The rangers clapped Joey and Chad obsequiously on the back and completely ignored me.

The climb up to Camp Muir was slow because Joey was sick, and we kept pace with him. Every time I'd been on that blasted mountain I'd climbed with someone who wasn't well. I'd thought this was my chance to find out what it *should* feel like to climb Mt. Rainier, but it wasn't meant to be.

There was plenty of room to set up our high camp because it was early in the climbing season and few people were up there. Chad and I shared his big tent, and Joey was in his own. I was sound asleep in my sleeping bag, but woke up with Chad snuggling up against me in a more than friendly manner. It was pitch dark and I sat up and said, "What the hell do you think you're doing?"

He said, "It's cold in here. I'm just trying to get warm."

"Bullshit, Chad! Get back on your side of the tent." He moved away, and I dropped back off. Chad was very happily married, according to some members in mountain rescue.

We got up at midnight to attempt the summit. The sky was clear, and we roped up and headed off. Everything went okay until we got to Disappointment Cleaver. We'd only seen two other men that night. They passed us as we started up the rocky cleaver, and then Chad told Joey and me to stay put while he assessed the route ahead. That scared me because I thought we might be lost. It occurred to me that if we got lost on the cleaver, we'd probably be stuck and not get out of that quagmire until daylight. I imagined I'd look very unattractive frozen solid. We all lucked out when another group of climbers straightened us out.

I was aware of the sunrise, but had no real interest in it on that climb, because I was half frozen. I'd hoped to warm up as we moved quickly to the summit, but as it turned out the ascent from the cleaver to the crater rim was interminable. Joey must've held the world's record for the smallest bladder, as we stopped while he rested, drank water and peed so many times that I lost count. His bladder control was worse than a pregnant woman's and I wanted to grab that water bottle right out of his hands and smack him over the head with it.

By the time we reached the crater rim, I was so cold I wished I wasn't there. My fingers and toes were numb, and I'd lost all interest in the summit a while ago. I wanted to get the hell off of that mountain and find some warmth. Tears seeped out of my eyes, and I complained that my hands and feet felt awfully cold. Chad, my snuggly tent mate, got Joey to help him warm them up on their stomachs. Then two guys who descended from the top passed by us and gave me a look of disgust. I was informed that I wouldn't be allowed to descend until Joey got the summit under his belt, and I wasn't surprised to hear that, because losing your spirit on a climb is no reason to turn around.

We all managed to get home in one piece after that climb. Oddly, Chad claimed in an OMR newsletter that his actions had saved me from stage two hypothermia on that climb. That was puzzling news to me.

Had he really thought I suffered from hypothermia? If so, then why did he keep me up there? Could prolonged exposure in below freezing temperatures be a new treatment?

I'm sure that Chad, with his hero status, got what he wanted, and Joey definitely got what he wanted, as he stood on the summit of Mt. Rainier. I didn't get what I wanted and found the entire experience irritating. The mountain brother idea didn't work and was crap. No one in my family would've laid a hand on me in the tent. Despite all that, I still had a shred of hope left and wanted to climb that blasted mountain with a healthy, competent climbing party someday.

Months later I was hiking and snowshoeing, but not finding climbing partners, as usual. That winter I'd spent several days trying to locate a climber to go up Mt. Ellinor with me. Whether it was my abrasive personality or because it was awfully cold out, I don't know, but try as I might no one wanted to go. Sensible people would take one look at the weather report and pull the blankets up over their heads. They'd rather stay at home through the long, cold and dreary winter, but I wasn't a fair weather climber and really needed to get out and up.

I packed the essentials: crampons, and my snowshoes, but couldn't find my brother's photo. I tore my pack apart, crawled around on the closet floor and turned my truck inside out. He was gone! I got really upset, then was sad, but thought, well I do have a lot of other pictures of him. I found one of the two of us when I was seven and he was nine, put it in a small plastic bag I'd gotten a necklace in and added a pink metallic heart. His picture had been my good luck talisman, and I hoped this one would work too.

On December 10, 2003, I stopped at the ranger station to see if they had a report on the current conditions at Mt. Ellinor. They didn't, but told me some people had gone up on the sixth. I assured them I'd do an avalanche assessment and give them a report on my way out.

I think the fact that I was wearing my red cold weather cap, with the Olympic Mountain Rescue emblem on it, increased their enthusiasm for my report. I sure got a lot of smiles.

I took the winter climber's route up to the chute. In the meadow approaching it there was about three feet of loose snow. One creek was still running, so I hopped over it, then did a quick avalanche assessment at the base of the chute. It looked stable, so with my ice axe in hand I kick stepped up the chute. Then out of the blue, another solo climber and his dog appeared! I wasn't expecting to see anyone up there that day. The other climber was a little older than my son Matt and told me his name was Andy. He occasionally called to his dog, Duke. That made me think of John Wayne. Duke was his nickname, and he was famous for saying "The hell I won't." One climber I'd invited to join me that day had told me I shouldn't go up there and I should've said that to him.

Andy, Duke, and I got above the chute. There was some ice in the bowl between the chute and the top of the peak. We tramped across the ice, headed to the summit, then began a slick, icy ascent. Finally I told Andy that I'd intended to turn around at about one o'clock. It was already 1:30 and cutting steps in ice was absolutely the last thing on earth I wanted to do, so I turned back. I didn't see him for a while, but he passed me on the way down and said he'd made the summit. I said "Great," with enthusiasm, but was a little jealous.

Going down the chute was a kick! Huge plunge steps had worked on that descent and I was transformed into Wonder Woman. I gave my avalanche assessment to the rangers, and they scribbled it down and thanked me. I'd started out at six in the morning and was home before dinner time. My climbing itch was scratched, and I felt like I was on top of the world.

The holidays passed by, leaving me with only the sad memory of Clint, and the new year crawling by in dark gloomy weather. Even though snowshoeing at Hurricane Ridge was beautiful, it wasn't even in the ballpark with climbing. Lillith was on my mind as a potential climbing partner, so I gave her a call and she arranged a climb on Mt.Washington with Cebe and me.

Saturday morning I was running late, so I skipped breakfast, got into my winter duds and was right on time at Cebe's, but Lil wasn't there. Cebe offered a cup of coffee, and I gladly accepted.

"Is Lillith still on board?"

"She's on board until she tells me she isn't, and I haven't heard from her."

We heard car wheels crunching on the gravel in Cebe's driveway. He looked out the kitchen window and announced, "She's here."

As I walked around the butcher block to peer out the window, she came bounding in. Lillith is a force of nature and was only a few minutes late. When I saw what she'd brought, she could have been 20 minutes late, and I wouldn't have minded one bit! She had a basket of freshly-baked blueberry muffins still warm, and a large pump pot of coffee. We hugged and Cebe said, "Lillith, you come bearing gifts!"

"Yes Cebe. I want to make sure we all get off on the right boot." I grabbed a muffin and inhaled it. They were heavenly and I gave her the thumbs up. Cebe looked up at his Felix the Cat clock.

"Well, I hate to interrupt breakfast, but we have to get this show on the road. Let's take these goodies with us and enjoy them on the way."

The hike from the car to the base of Mt. Washington was a short one. Each time I'd climbed that peak it was always hard to find the start in the winter due to heavy snow, but it was springtime then. Even though it wasn't as congested with snow, we all got tired of looking for a good place to start up, and just plowed in through the woods. When we came out onto the snowfield, the snow was as bad as it gets. It was wet and mushy. Talk about post holing! With each step we sank six to twelve inches deep, and I was glad I'd brought my trekking poles.

Cebe apologized for the crummy snow, as though he was responsible for it, and told us it would either get better soon or we'd have to turn around. It didn't get better, and the post holes were getting deeper. Cebe decided we should try it another day. I was in the middle with Cebe in the lead and Lillith was right behind me.

As we descended I tried to follow Cebe closely, and when I stepped into one of his bootprints, my right leg sank into the snow right up to my thigh, and that leg felt like it was stuck. I jerked up and back and tried to pull it out, and was overcome with paroxysms of pain. I was crying and holding onto my leg, and Lillith was right by my side.

"What happened? Are you okay?"

"No. Do I look okay?" My right boot had twisted under a branch or something and my leg was stuck. It was the same knee I'd injured years ago. I tried again to pull it out and it twisted. That must've really screwed it up because it reminded me of the pain I'd felt when I blew it out skiing in Virginia.

Cebe asked, "Paula, do you think you can walk out?" He handed me his hanky.

Tears and snot were streaming down my face. I blubbered," I don't know."

Lillith was Johnny on the spot with her bandanna as a compress. I put my arms around their shoulders, and we gingerly picked our way down the mountain. We had to go into the woods, and I was afraid I wouldn't be able to manage it, but somehow did.

At the car, Cebe gave me Ibuprofen, and Lillith packed snow around my knee then wrapped the bandanna around it. My leg was elevated in the car, and poor Lil had my foot nearly in her face.

I made it home in one piece from that climb on Washington and had to take a few days off from work. The knee gradually felt better, and

I gave a lot of thought to whether or not I should continue to climb. I decided that since my knee was much better, and was just a little stiff, that I should be able to pursue my favorite sport.

One day as I walked downstairs, I heard a clicking sound coming from that knee. I consulted with an osteopath and was scheduled for surgery. The doctor scoped it, but didn't repair it. He told me he hadn't been able to find anything that he could fix and told me that my knee was past the point of repair, and my next surgery would be a knee replacement.

That doctor was considered to be one of the top ten surgeons in Seattle (I'd done my homework before I made an appointment with him). He pronounced the sentence that I could no longer run, climb, do power yoga or any heavy lifting. Since I knew I didn't need a second opinion, I realized that Mt. Washington had been my first and last alpine climb, and basically I was screwed.

Everything that I'd loved to do had been taken away from me. I'd been told to replace the most thrilling and exuberant activities with the incredibly dull prospect of taking a walk! I'd compare that to breaking a horse's leg, but not shooting it and then expecting it to have a good quality of life. I wasn't ready to be put out of my misery, but was completely miserable. The world had gone from kaleidoscopic full color to a blurry gray.

Since that surgery had only been arthroscopic, it healed quickly. About 6 months later, my friend Bryan invited me to rock climb with him and some of his friends. Sailing with him a couple of years before had been a rush and we'd talked about climbing, but never seemed to get around to it. I didn't want to tell him that my climbing days were over, so I said I'd look at my work schedule and call him back later. Any sort of climbing had been strictly forbidden, but I wanted to go so badly, and my knee felt good. I decided to do it and called back to confirm the trip. That rock climb at the gorge would be my last-gasp climb before I put all my gear in storage. Nobody — not even my doctor — would stop me.

Bryan and I camped at Frenchman Coulee and the next day were met by his friends, a couple in their thirties. Two short pitches on the Feathers were about all I could handle when my knee rebelled in pain. I didn't say a word to Bryan and hoped it would subside. We all headed over to the Sunshine Wall after lunch.

My rack was slung across my body, it clanked and jangled as I hiked. Two climbers walked toward me and one of them slowed down to check out my rack — by which I mean the trad pro on my sling. My knee pain was increasing, and I'd just begun to limp, when I remembered something Jack Kerouac once said. "Pain or Love or Danger makes you real again." The man who slowed down to inspect my gear whistled softly and said, "Wow, you must be a pretty good climber." I just gave him a smile because I knew I had been.

# ACKNOWLEDGEMENTS

||||||||||||||||||||||||||||||||||||||||||||||||||||||||||||||||||||||||||||||||||||||||

THANK YOU TO my dear friend Cebe Wallace for introducing me to mountaineering and some of the best times I've had in my life. Many thanks to Nancy Rekow for her suggestions about my writing style. Thank you Rob Bignell for editing the fifth draft. I want to thank Jan and Dale Boyle for teaching me to trad climb. I also want to thank my friend and neighbor Carol Chu, who inspired me to write this book. Thanks to Diane Brintzenhofe and Brenda DiPrete who encouraged me and read my rough drafts. I especially want to thank my three sons Matt Elling, Willy and Max Ingersoll who all managed to put up with me during my climbing obsession. Last but not least, a big shout out to my climbing brother John Ellsworth.

# ABOUT THE AUTHOR

||||||||||||||||||||||||||||||||||||||||||||||||||||||||||||||||||||||||||||||

PAULA ENGBORG GAINED all her climbing expertise in the school of hard knocks. She's the proud mother of 3 handsome men, and her occupations ranged from serving in the U.S. Army Military Police to running her own company Fit for Life, on Bainbridge Island, WA. After she retired, Paula finally got around to going to college in her 50's and has an associates degree in technical arts from Olympic College. This is her first book.

# OIL ON WATER PRESS
## True-Life Stories and Memoir

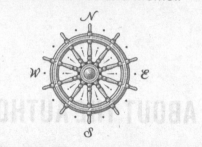

**THE TOWN SLOWLY EMPTIES: On Life and Culture during Lockdown by Manash Firaq Bhattacharjee** A latter-day Journal of the Plague Year. The author rekindles ties with culture, and affirms friendship, empathy and love.
pbk 978-1-909394-75-9 / 978-1-909394-76-6

**SMALL TOWN SKATEPARKS by Clint Carrick** A skateboarding road trip celebrating the institution of the skatepark in America's small towns.
pbk 978-1-909394-77-3 / ebk 978-1-909394-78-0

**A BROOKLYN MEMOIR: My Life as a Boy by Robert Rosen** Brooklyn, 1955–64: A Jewish boy learns about life and death from the W.W. II vets and Holocaust survivors who surround him.
pbk 978-1-909394-98-8 / ebk 978-1-909394-99-5

**HEAVY METAL HEADBANG by Melissa Meszaros** After being hit by a car on the way to a Judas Priest concert, Melissa Meszaros' life is turned upside down by a traumatic brain injury.
pbk 978-1-909394-85-8 / ebk 978-1-909394-86-5

**LETTING GO THE LEASH by Stephen Ellis Hamilton** Redemptive tale set against a tornado and a pandemic. Banker Stephen Ellis Hamilton quits his job of thirty-four years to save a rescue dog. And himself.
pbk 978-1-909394-87-2 / ebk 978-1-909394-88-9

**A WAY UP: 1 Woman Across the Pacific NW by Paula Engborg** An energetic, 41-year-old divorcee in search of Prince Charming one day finds a new sport: The Climb. Paula Engborg has barely ascended a stepladder, so why the desire to climb mountains?
pbk 978-1-909394-89-6 / ebk 978-1-909394-90-2

**WALK THIS WAY by Duncan McNamara** The Way is a pilgrim trail that runs 500 miles west from the French foothills of the Pyrenees to the Shrine of St James the Great. Following the death of his father, Duncan McNamara sets off with a rucksack of mostly useless items on an unusual adventure.
[*Published September 2023*]
pbk 978-1-915316-25-7 / ebk 978-1-915316-26-4

oilonwaterpress.com